UNENDING DIALOGUE

UNENDING DIALOGUE

Voices from an AIDS Poetry Workshop

BY

RACHEL HADAS

*With Charles Barber, Glenn Besco,
Dan Conner, Tony J. Giordano,
Kevin Imbusch, Glenn Philip Kramer,
Raul Martinez-Avila, and
James Turcotte*

FOREWORD BY TIM SWEENEY,
GAY MEN'S HEALTH CRISIS

Faber and Faber
BOSTON • LONDON

Copyright © 1991 by Rachel Hadas
Foreword copyright © 1991 by Tim Sweeney
The acknowledgments on p. xi constitute an extension of this copyright notice

Library of Congress Cataloging-in-Publication Data

Hadas, Rachel.
    Unending dialogue : voices from an AIDS poetry workshop / by Rachel Hadas with Charles Barber . . . [et. al.].
        p.   cm.
    ISBN 0-571-12943-9 (cloth) : $17.95
    1. AIDS (Disease)—Poetry.   2. American poetry—20th century.
    3. Gays' writings, American.   4. Gay men—poetry.   I. Title.
PS595.A36H33   1991
811'.54080356—dc20   91—18823
                                                                            CIP

Cover design by Don Leeper
Photograph by Jennifer Y. Cheung

Printed in the United States of America

To my coauthors,
with admiration and love

Contents

Foreword

IN HER OPENING ESSAY, Rachel Hadas turns her poet's ear to the strange ring of the acronyms that have gained currency in the decade of AIDS. First on her list is GMHC—Gay Men's Health Crisis—an organization whose acronym is now familiar to many Americans whose lives have been changed by the AIDS epidemic. For the unfamiliar reader, the poems that Ms. Hadas has included in this collection—and the story of the poetry workshop that generated many of them—go far in communicating the powerful language of hope and loss that has come with the AIDS epidemic. For those of us working at GMHC, the book is a poetic rendering of what lies behind our acronym, a spelling out of the most basic principles informing our fight against AIDS.

Willingness to work with what you have is one such principle. Gay Men's Health Crisis was founded in 1981 by a small group of gay men who passed the hat to help sick friends cope with the mysterious disease we now know as AIDS. We have grown into the world's largest AIDS service organization by asking that everyone—gay, straight, HIV-infected or not—step forward and volunteer what they can to fight the ravages of the worst health care crisis in modern history. Rachel Hadas came forward with her skills as a poet and teacher to lead a poetry workshop. As with many volunteers, she learned as well as taught.

Unending Dialogue achieves something all GMHC programs strive for: it allows people with AIDS their own voice. There is perhaps no more instructive, or radical, approach to raising consciousness about a disease whose realities are clouded in moralizing and stigma. The poems that emerge— from the lyrical vision of AIDS drug administration expressed by "13 Things about a Catheter" to the terser, more frightened "The Storm"—form a powerful collection of work that is as varied as the clients that pass through GMHC's doors every day.

This book does not offer the last word, or poem, on AIDS. With over 100,000 Americans now dead from AIDS, the epidemic continues to spread. As the caseloads of GMHC and other community-based AIDS organizations rise steadily, government on all levels is failing to provide sufficient funds, or leadership, to our fight. New voices are rising to ask for greater access to health care, more AIDS prevention education, and better AIDS research. New poems are being written. The dialogue, as Rachel Hadas has noted, is far from over.

Tim Sweeney
Executive Director
Gay Men's Health Crisis
New York

Acknowledgments

Some of the contents of this book have been previously published, as follows:

"The Lights Must Never Go Out" was published in *Threepenny Review*, Spring 1989, and in *Living in Time* (New Brunswick: Rutgers University Press, 1990).

"The Lenten Tunnel" appeared in *Poets for Life: Seventy-five Poets Respond to AIDS*, edited by Michael Klein (New York: Crown, 1989).

"Elegy Variations," Part I ("Tears") appeared in *The American Scholar*, Summer 1989.

"The Revenant" appeared in *Threepenny Review*, Summer 1990.

"Less Than Kind" is forthcoming in *Denver Quarterly*, 1991–2.

"Laments" won Second Prize in the Ann Stanford Poetry Contest, Writing Program, University of Southern California at San Diego, March 1990, and was published in *The Southern California Anthology*, Volume VIII, Summer 1990.

"Fin de Siècle" appeared in *The New Republic*, issue 3989, July 1, 1991.

"Conversation by the Body's Light," copyright © 1977 by Jane Cooper, is reprinted from *Scaffolding: New and Selected Poems* by permission of the author and Anvil Press Poetry Ltd.

All poems by members of the GMHC workshop are printed by permission of the authors.

I want to thank Gay Men's Health Crisis, in particular Daniel Brewer of Recreation, for wonderful support; the late Mark Corrodi for his inspiring collage; Mike Loud for his photographs. Also, John Heuston for his superb typing and Betsy Uhrig of Faber and Faber for her faith in me, her unerring taste, and her unfailing enthusiasm.

I

THE LIGHTS MUST
NEVER GO OUT

The Lights Must Never Go Out

GMHC. PWA. CMP. KS. PCP. The endless acronyms reminded me of POUM and the other political parties Orwell speaks of in *Homage to Catalonia*. A harmless phenomenon, maybe; an insider's lingo to which one gets accustomed with inconceivable rapidity. AIDS itself is an acronym, after all. No one else at the three-day training session for Gay Men's Health Crisis (GMHC) volunteers seemed to mind.

But the aggressively bureaucratic way in which acronyms appropriated words, so that the tasks of daily living become TDL's, gave me the creeps. Nor was it only the acronyms. The term care management partner (CMP), for example, was a phrase that seemed to institutionalize, by sheathing it in official sounding jargon, a person or people whose very existence might be contingent, undependable, or nonexistent.

One of the first things we prospective volunteers were taught was to eschew the words "patient" and "victim." One spoke of a person with AIDS, a PWA (and since AIDS-related complex becomes ARC, there are also PWArcs); any PWA coming to the agency (as GMHC often refers to itself) is a client. Nancy Reagan, we were reminded, wasn't being referred to in the press as a cancer patient or victim, but as a person with cancer.

I could see the point of this practice; but I couldn't help being reminded of the way "pain," as in labor pain, was a taboo term during natural childbirth classes. Instead, one said "contraction," a word which didn't exactly prepare me for the reality of giving birth.

It's not surprising that the relation of words to reality was (as they say in the trade) an issue for me: the reason I was at the training session was that I wanted to set up a poetry workshop for PWA's in the Recreation Center of GMHC. Calling things by their true names seems to me to be one of the functions of poetry; was I a saboteur from the start? Another volunteer at Recreation, who ran an art group, told me of his initial fears of physical contact with clients, and such fears are common. My own fears were a lot more recondite; they all had to do with what I perceived as the ambiguous if not contradictory nature of my project. Assuming I could get a poetry workshop going, that even a few PWA's would be interested; assuming the workshop "worked" well enough for poetry to exercise its mysterious power of truth-telling; well, was this what the clients needed or wanted? Or would I merely, in one of my father's favorite phrases, be filling a much-needed gap?

This was hardly the kind of anxiety the training session was designed to address. Indeed, during the three long days of various kinds of presentations, very little was specifically directed toward volunteers who wanted to work in the area of recreation, for the good reason that other branches of GMHC, such as financial aid, were a lot more crucial. Nevertheless, a repeated theme was the emotional complexities and ambiguities inherent in this kind of volunteer work. We were urged to be introspective, to examine our own needs and motivations. If you find yourself getting too involved with your clients, warned a theatrically charming young man, watch out — that's not a volunteer job, that's a life-style. Yet the last talk, at the end of the third day — the tale we were apparently supposed to carry home with us — was a lengthy, increasingly teary account by a young woman of her year with her client. It was undeniably an odd kind of love story (he loved Jerry Lewis movies, she hated them; she tried to encourage him to read, he wouldn't), but a love story it was. By the time he died, Richie had become, if not exactly her life-style, a devoted audience of her life, as she of his. The story left us with a sense of overwhelming mutual need, and even mutual fulfillment, between this client and his CMP. Was it a cautionary tale, or was the tearful volunteer some kind of role model for us novices?

Perhaps both. Sooner or later one notices the thoroughgoing doubleness of almost any meaning. It seemed to me, for example, that the act of volunteering at GMHC was tantamount to an admission that my husband and son, my teaching and writing, my students and friends combined still didn't quite fill all my time and energy — put differently, didn't fill my needs. At times this seemed to mean that I had a lot of energy, a lot to give and a need to give it; at other times, that I was in search of a balm, looking to cure a shameful residue of emptiness and loneliness. This double perspective could be disconcerting, but I learned to live with it.

Much more troublesome was the way in which, as I've said, the very idea of the workshop seemed paradoxical. The whole thing was my idea; no one was making me do it; yet I couldn't help envisioning any poetry group with PWA's as an uncomfortable alternation of compassion and stimulus — a use of poetry both to soothe and to prod. Never having thought of myself as the nurturing type, I knew I was no Florence Nightingale (I also certainly lack her formidable organizational talent); but I kept remembering another redoubtable, if fictional, Victorian volunteer. Mrs. Pardiggle, one of an unforgettable gallery of philanthropists in Dickens's *Bleak House*, makes house calls in order to hand out little moral tracts to brickmakers who are not only desperately poor and sick but also illiterate. Not that I expected my clients to be illiterate. It was not knowing what to expect that made my imagination so fertile.

If the Mrs. Pardiggle model had proved an accurate forecast, I doubt if I'd be writing this. Of course the workshop, when it started, was very different from what I'd pictured. It would be wonderful to be able to report that a large, enthusiastic, and cohesive group of talented poets formed immediately, wrote prolifically, and gave each other strength and inspiration week by week; but the reality, as it unfolded between January and May, was a lot more fragmentary and hesitant than that. To begin with, the "group" was and remained tiny; never more than four men, often only two, and sometimes one. There were various reasons for this, among them the very limited publicity GMHC was able to give new activities. Accustomed to the comfortable institutional umbrella that had always been provided by Rutgers, where I teach, or by well-established poetry programs such as the Ninety-second Street Y, I found I very much didn't want to have to market my nebulous wares, buttonholing the quiet men at the Recreation Center to talk up the power of poetry. The workshop was listed in the Recreation Center's newsletter and calendar, and I eventually learned enough to put a notice in the PWA Coalition Newsline, an indispensable monthly. Word of mouth also worked—slowly. But the main reason for the smallness of the group was certainly the limited attraction of poetry for most people.

Smallness was fine. But it meant that such dynamic metaphors as building up momentum, getting off the ground, perhaps even getting going were inappropriate. We weren't a jet plane or a corporation. As Gustavo, my friend from the training session, reminded me, the point was to be process-oriented.

What was this process like? My expectations (as opposed to my Mrs. Pardiggle fears) had been vaguely based on my past experiences of weekly poetry classes or workshops where much of the hour was devoted to discussing one or two people's poems, xeroxed copies of which had been passed around. And there was a classroom feel to the proceedings. When it came to giving assignments, suggesting revisions, endlessly editing, I wasn't a bit shy.

But that first Friday afternoon there were only two men waiting for me, and one of them said he'd love to chat but didn't feel like writing. So I had a "class" of one—with one observer? The three of us did a lot of talking about family, jobs, and holidays (this was shortly after Christmas); after a while, as I'll describe in a minute, we circled closer to the subject of AIDS.

The amount of chitchat was to be a constant. I sometimes felt like the composition teacher who was one of my husband's favorite college professors and who spent about forty-five minutes out of every hour and a half class fooling around before getting down to work. The smallness of the groups made it easier to be informal (also, sometimes, easier to work intensively); my image of a class was superseded by that of a tutorial. Teacher and student, heads bent over the text, preparing for an imminent exam; two students cramming together, tossing ideas back and forth, testing each other—both these mordant analogies occurred to me at different times.

Every teacher knows that if the students are good, small classes can work beautifully. At one session, each of the two students/clients/PWA's, henceforth to be called by their own names, did some free writing, a technique I'll describe; then they exchanged papers, and each chose a line or phrase from the other man's work that he particularly liked, and tried to work it into his own developing poem. One phrase of Kevin's that Wayne chose, "the light at the end of the Lenten tunnel," has stayed with me; I've borrowed it too. Kevin's favorite phrase from Wayne's work was something about crying in the dark; I was reminded of Tennyson's *In Memoriam* ("An infant crying in the night/An infant crying for the light/And with no language but a cry."). We were able to check the reference because I'd brought along my trusty anthology; it had become clear that reading, as much as writing, was the purpose of the workshop.

Wayne also liked Kevin's phrase, "rich in hope," that I was quick to point out was itself a borrowing from Shakespeare's Sonnet 29:

> Wishing me like to one more rich in hope,
> Featured like him, like him of friends possessed,
> Desiring this man's art and that man's scope,
> With what I most enjoy contented least.

Kevin knew he was borrowing; knew the poem, though like me he couldn't remember how that sonnet began. So much for the cultural level of at least some of my clients. I hadn't had to worry about being a Mrs. Pardiggle; the hostile brickmakers had voted with their feet. Perhaps the closest I ever came to them was the hour I spent with a vivacious and beautiful black transvestite, who wanted to write, hoped to make money by writing, and indeed did write a little poem, but whose writing was at about a third grade level. Still, David (or Traci; s/he said I could use either name) was anything but hostile.

Not everyone works well in pairs. Kevin, who worked well with Wayne, never took to Paul; Paul, intense and industrious, was rewarding to work with one on one but dealt with the presence of others by ignoring them. Bill used to sit in apparent abstraction, not commenting on other people's work; yet he always asked to hear what they had written, and himself wrote plangent, delicate poems in an almost illegible scrawl.

As the weeks went by, I got more of a sense of the atmosphere of the Recreation Center—a loft on Twenty-third Street in which my poetry operation took up an understandably tiny corner. Gradually, a better analogy than either classroom or tutorial suggested itself, and as an added bonus threw a shaft of light on some of my reasons for being at GMHC.

Some time ago, I spent several years on the Greek island of Samos. I was very struck there, until I got used to it, by the amount of time men of all ages seemed to spend sitting around in one of the village's three or four coffeehouses, discussing the news of today or yesterday or twenty years ago or just twirling their worry beads, smoking cigarettes, and surveying the passing scene. An anomalous detail of that scene was, of course, my presence. Since I knew the language pretty well, during my time in the village I was a more or less accepted sojourner in an almost wholly male environment. (The world of the women, behind the doors of their houses, seemed a lot more private and impenetrable; if I'd had a child I would have had more access to that world.) Without sharing all the men's concerns, I was conversant with many of them. Not that I deceived myself that I was one of them. I always could, and finally did, get up and leave the world of endlessly unfolding *kotsombolió* (gossip's a pale translation)—just as I could leave the world of GMHC—and never come back.

Something powerfully attracted me to both these seemingly alien worlds. Partly, I think it was the privileged status of the outsider who not only observes but who can also minimally participate in the action, or at least in the conversation, without untoward responsibility—a kind of benign playacting? Certainly I used to find myself thinking of the coffeehouse gatherings as endless rehearsals which merged imperceptibly into equally open-ended performances. Another attraction, since I'd finished college soon before coming to Greece, was what I then saw as the enviable wealth of time the denizens of the cafés seemed to have at their disposal. Each day was a mild variation on the day before; it seemed to stretch from six A.M. or so till after dark, with space for a siesta; the harbor frieze changed like a slow motion kaleidoscope, and the old men, part of it themselves, watched and commented. Sometimes someone would call out to me as I scurried past on some errand: "Why are you in such a hurry?" They seemed to me, and maybe to themselves, to have all the time in the world. It didn't occur to me then that most of their time was behind them.

Here in this Chelsea loft fifteen years after I'd left Greece were round tables, with small clumps of men sitting, smoking, drinking coffee, reading the paper, chatting . . . watching the passing scene. In one corner were sofas and a TV; a group dozed or lounged and watched the soaps in a desultory way. In the central kitchen area, a man in an apron was chopping broccoli. A constant slow coming and going took place; people inquired how X was, who had seen Y, what was the news of Z. New York City roared by outside the windows, but in here no one was in a rush. For people whom time was killing, the best revenge was to kill time in return—slowly, slowly.

Perhaps it's perverse, then, that one of the things we did in the workshop was write against the clock. Free writing, a technique described by, among others, Peter Elbow in *Writing without Teachers*, is a way for writers (and not only beginners) to banish writer's block, to vanquish the specter of the inspired piece of writing that comes out perfectly on the first try. One sim-

7

ply writes, for five or ten or fifteen minutes or as long as one can stand it, without stopping at all, without even taking one's hand off the page. What to write about? Write nonsense, write loops and squiggles if you have to, but don't stop.

Sometimes the process is merely a warm-up. With luck, though, some subject uncovers itself as you go—enough of a subject so that it's possible to extract a fleck of gold from the ore when you look back at what you've written. Some people took to free writing with a kind of starved intensity; others wanted more direction, and being less draconian than Peter Elbow I was happy to accommodate them. Kenneth Koch's anthology *Sleeping on the Wing* has wonderful suggestions for imitating certain characteristics of the poems included in the collection. In Emily Dickinson's "I Heard a Fly Buzz," for example, what interests Koch is not Dickinson's formal peculiarities but the way she focuses on a specific sensation in the face of death's enormity. Since Dickinson's poem is short and comparatively easy to assimilate, it provided a good model for a variant on free, or at any rate in-class, writing. (I was always tempted to give assignments from week to week, but it was a measure of the aorist mode of the place that while future pleasures could be talked about, things had to be done now.)

Here are two imitations of "I Heard a Fly Buzz" written by men in the workshop. True to Koch's emphasis, they pay more attention to Dickinson's vision than to her metrical or rhythmical patterns. Neither is a slavish copy; one is relaxed enough to sprout a second stanza.

> The day I was diagnosed
> the fan blew coolly upon me
> From the window vent the fan
> hushed me up. And I forgot
> for the moment that it
> was I who was slowly blowing away.

and

> The phone was ringing when the World Ended
> the first ring startled—will Someone please answer it—
> I'm busy—I have to finish this—
> this must be completed before it all ends—
> Will someone Please answer that—
> I have to show that I have lived—I have to prove my worth—
>
> That Incessant ringing—why don't they hang up—
> I'm Busy—I have to Finish this—
> the Room is shaking—It's almost Over—
> Why does it Keep ringing—

I have to complete this—I have to show that I Am—
I'll get it—Hello— Hello— Hello— No one there—
I have to Finish this—I have to prove I lived—

Glenn, who added the second stanza at home, has of course paid close attention to Dickinson's unorthodox punctuation and capitalization; but it's interesting that Dickinson's buzzing fly turns into a characteristically twentieth-century convenience (fan, phone) in each of these poems.

Sometimes a casual suggestion could set someone off. Kevin was taken by the title of the newly published Garcia Marquez novel *Love in the Time of Cholera*, and suggested "Love in a Time of Plague" as a good title for a poem. (Kevin, one of those writers who's better at starting projects than at finishing them, had a knack for getting other people to work on tasks that were stumping him. I found myself not only trying to write poems on some of the topics he suggested, but even assigning some of these topics to my writing students at Rutgers.) Bill, who rarely spoke, wrote for a few minutes and handed me this poem to read aloud:

> Love in a time of plague
> is like:
> finding roses on the moon
> or fish in the desert
> or oysters on the grass
> or daisies on the moon
> there is no love in time of plague
> only fear, destruction
> And yet I love you, this time of plague
> or do I love the plague
> and not you
> I do not know if I confuse plague and
> love. Both are fatal, infectious, cause for
> concern. And yet, if I could
> choose, I'd choose to love you
> and find my roses on the moon.

I hope these examples make it clear that for those who chose to come to the workshop, many of the materials of poetry were there —above all an urgent theme. The question was hardly ever *what*, as it so often is in the kind of workshop excoriated by the poet and critic Donald Hall, where poetry is a parlor game. For men with AIDS (I'd like to write "suffering from AIDS," but I don't want to fight City Hall), the what was a given—was for much of the time *the* given of their daily lives. Their presence at the workshop, at the Recreation Center, indeed their having come to GMHC in the first place was a gesture of need, exactly as my presence every Friday was, at least in part, an admission of reciprocal need.

The problem wasn't one of subject matter, themes, ideas, experience — rather it was a question of techniques for getting a purchase on material that could be so overwhelming as to be either incommunicable or, of all things, banal. I didn't ask the men to produce great art, but I hoped to find a focus, an intensity. Czeslaw Milosz is referring to something like this struggle when he writes in *The Witness of Poetry*:

> Some detachment, some coldness is necessary to elaborate a form. People thrown into the middle of events that tear cries of pain from their mouths have difficulty in finding the distance to transform this material artistically.

That first Friday, after a good deal of small talk I started to edge closer to what brought us (the three of us, as it happened) there. Sidling in where, so far as I knew, angels feared to tread, I spoke of the disease. If I were in their shoes, I said to the men, I'd be angry.

I thought I was telling the truth that day, but I think I know better now. Anger, like many strong emotions, is transitory, sporadic, and exhausting. It demands and fuels energy; it also uses energy up. The men facing me seemed more gentle and tired than anything else. (It occurs to me now that Bill's little poem about the way the fan distracted him from his diagnosis expresses an important fact about the lability of our powers of concentration, especially when what we're trying to concentrate on is horrible, but even if it's not. Grace Paley, in another context, puts it this way: "I cannot keep my mind on Jerusalem / It wanders off like an idiot with no attention span / to whatever city lies outside my window that day . . . ")

Be that as it may, Jay (who didn't feel like writing) and Wayne politely agreed that yes, they were angry. Frustrated rather than angry, qualified Jay, who had trouble getting around. Wayne had lesions like bruises under his eyes, and it made him angry, he said, when people stared at him on the street or asked him where he got his black eye. We talked some more, mostly about faces and people's curiosity, as I recall. At some point Wayne handed me a scrapbook of earlier poems he had brought along. I had a chance to look at it right away, because Wayne suddenly started writing in an almost virgin notebook. He had remembered something.

A lot of Wayne's earlier work was celebratory, occasional, markedly upbeat. There were several poems about Alaska, where his work as a tap dancer performing on a cruise ship had taken him. My favorite piece in the scrapbook was a prose tribute to a man named Henry, who seemed to have been both a choreographer and Wayne's teacher. I liked the nervous energy with which Wayne wrote about energy:

. . . the glorious times of working together. Henry puffing on his cigarette and pacing the floor—with me anxious and ready to learn whatever it was that came out. He was like a pressure cooker. When working on a project, he barely slept. The music played over and over in his head and he paced. Then he would start with you—one step at a time—creating something extraordinary. It was sensational—my nerves tingled on the surface as the patterns unfolded before me. It was like a puzzle being unlocked in Henry's brain.

What Wayne was scribbling today turned out to be altogether darker: not a farewell tribute to a respected teacher who had "a gift for the world," but the beginning of a farewell to a more difficult proposition: himself.

As if I'd been lecturing on Eliot's notion of the objective correlative instead of asking vague questions about anger, Wayne had pounced on a memory of a recent morning, when he was taking a shower:

> In the midst of soaping my body
>   to start the day automatically
> I turn and catch a view of me
>   in the mirror—
>   dying . . .
>   a look of death
>   that lies around the eyes
>   in pale taut skin
>   against the bones.
> I want to reach out and soothe
>   the anger and sadness of the man
>   there in the mirror.

For the next two months, Wayne worked on this poem. With a few hints from me, he found ways to articulate the various short segments that kept emerging into a sequence of visions of himself at different stages of his life, glimpsed through a series of mirrors.

Like many talented students, Wayne was grateful to a teacher who felt she had had next to nothing to do. (Did Henry feel about Wayne's dancing as I did about his writing?) I'm as indebted to Wayne as he was to me. His unfinished mirror poem came to signify that double power of poetry which so worried me when I thought of it as a contradiction between consoling and telling the truth. Wayne saw that soothing (he uses the word at the start of his poem) can be accomplished, not by denial, but by naming; not by looking away, but by taking courage to meet the eyes of the man in the mirror, even if that man is oneself, and is dying. For "me in the mirror . . . dying" was no poetic hyperbole; Wayne died in April, less than three months after I'd met him.

11

The way we can feel a person's presence intimately even after that person's death is a source of wonder and gratitude to me. Like the expanse of time stretching out behind the old men in the coffeehouses, this presence carried over from the past adds a dimension to a present that can feel impoverished and pinched simply because it is the present (in Robert Frost's words, "too present to imagine"). What is in human terms a precious gift is exactly what we often expect of poetry, what we take for granted when it's bestowed. Ensconced in an anthology, or better yet in memory, the poetry we love is permanently available, is not only there for us but part of us in a way no other person can be. It was on some such assumption that I soon began to use the workshop time for reading as well as writing. Auden and Shakespeare, Cavafy and Dickinson, Whitman and Stevens spoke louder than Wayne or Kevin or I could.

Yet even poems one knows by heart are strangely fugitive, slipping in and out of the memory and the affections. This nebulous and unpredictable quality is part of what Merleau-Ponty has in mind when he says that artistic expression "is like a step taken in the fog; no one can say where, if anywhere, it will lead." Poems can lose their intensity, their special appropriateness, at any moment, without warning—especially if they're being taught. But they may also, equally without warning, leap into focus, take on new dimensions of meaning.

GMHC provided a context I'd never imagined. Not surprisingly, I'd never given a thought to how incredibly apposite, how eloquent poems I'd loved for years would be in the light of AIDS. Not only the lives and deaths of young men, but details like the background music in the Recreation Center or my own moments of reticence seemed to have been understood and recorded by poets long dead. A few examples will have to suffice.

The spring of 1988 was a time of several successes for me—successes it seemed totally inappropriate to bring into the workshop. It would be hard for me to articulate the reason for not telling the men I saw on Fridays this or that piece of good news; fortunately, Robert Lowell in his poem on Robert Frost has recorded the older poet's sense of our human separateness. "I" is Lowell and "he" is Frost:

> And I: "Sometimes I'm so happy I can't stand myself."
> And he: "When I am too full of joy, I think
> how little good my health did anyone near me."

More important were passages that expressed with luminous inevitability—and one is tempted to add clairvoyance—what the men were experiencing. I remember showing Wayne and Kevin Auden's "Lullaby" as an example, first of assonance, and then, as we took the poem in, of a starkly unsentimental vision of love. The poem hit closer to home than that for

Wayne, who after his weekly chemotherapy was often sick in the night and who tried not to awaken his lover. The poem speaks for either or both of them:

> Time and fevers burn away
> Individual beauty from
> Thoughtful children, and the grave
> Proves the child ephemeral:
> But in my arms till break of day
> Let the living creature lie,
> Mortal, guilty, but to me
> The entirely beautiful.

Terry Eagleton says that Shakespeare has clearly read Marx, Husserl, Wittgenstein, Freud, Derrida. Just as clearly, Auden, as well as Whitman, Keats, and Cavafy, knew all about AIDS. Here is Auden again, ostensibly writing about a bar on Fifty-second Street in "September 1, 1939" but really thinking of the Recreation center loft, with its posters and video, its kitchen smells and its endless background music:

> The lights must never go out,
> The music must always play,
> All the conventions conspire
> To make this fort assume
> The furniture of home
> Lest we should see where we are,
> Lost in a haunted wood,
> Children afraid of the night
> Who have never been happy or good.

The light refuses to go out also for Theodore Roethke in his prescient, which is to say timeless, poem "In a Dark Time":

> I know the purity of pure despair,
> My shadow pinned against a sweating wall.
>
> A steady storm of correspondences!
> A night flowing with birds, a ragged moon,
> and in broad day the midnight come again!
> A man goes far to find out what he is—
> Death of the self in a long, tearless night,
> All natural shapes blazing unnatural light.

There are more passages, from Homer to Housman, that take on fresh poignance, and thus also fresh timelessness, from the situation of AIDS. Because poetry, despite the loudly proclaimed death of the author, is written by and for people, the resilience and adaptability shown in these startling leaps of relevance are reflections of the resilience and adaptability of what Wallace Stevens has called the never-resting mind. The AIDS crisis has created terrible suffering; it has also called forth the inventiveness and elasticity of human intelligence.

It isn't only poems that can leap suddenly into focus. In the work of two prose writers who mean a lot to me, I've recently come across—apparently by chance—passages that seem pregnant with significance for what I was attempting to do in the workshop. It's as well that I didn't come across the first passage back during the training session. Severely and perspicaciously, Proust declares that the artist has no business trying to make contact with the rest of the world:

> Authentic art has no use for proclamations, it accomplishes its work in silence. To be altogether true to his spiritual life an artist must remain alone and not be prodigal of himself even to disciples. . . . When human altruism is not egotistic it is sterile, as for instance in the writer who interrupts his work to visit an unfortunate friend, or to write propaganda articles.

Since I am a poet, this passage speaks eloquently to my desire and need for solitude, for a more contemplative, introspective life; it speaks to my distrust of poetry as a therapeutic tool, and even, perhaps, to my instinctive dislike of acronyms. If I were a writer of anything like Proust's stature, perhaps this admonition would be valid for me, and the whole idea of the workshop would be a misguided and self-serving waste of time.

But I am inextricably in the world already. As mother, as teacher I juggle my writing with other tasks which also matter to me, and I don't think my poetry suffers unconscionably from these distractions. In other words, despite an inevitable shortage of time, I feel less fragile than the obsessive artist that Proust was and whom he is depicting.

I don't feel fragile, but I do feel mortal—which gives me something in common with the "unfortunate friends" I encountered at GMHC. (Proust's artist, it could be argued, manages to escape the toils of mortality through sacrificing his worldly existence to his art.) And it is this commonality which the second passage addresses, as well as the simple fact that every writer is also (and was first) a reader. Two hours of altruism a week are selfishly well spent if they give me a fresh sense of what literature can do. Lighting up the human moment, poems become themselves illuminated in the process; and as a third step in a miraculous proliferation of energy, this illumination in turn serves, by linking the readers in shared wonder, to lessen human isolation.

This, anyhow, is what I get from the chapter entitled "The Canto of

Ulysses" in Primo Levi's *Survival in Auschwitz*. Levi's description of how the Ulysses Canto of Dante's *Inferno* came transcendently alive for him (and through him for a fellow prisoner) during his time in the concentration camp is itself a transcendent passage, and, though very concise, too long to quote fully here. The heart of the passage occurs when Levi, hurriedly translating whatever he can remember of the canto into French for the benefit of his companion, is overwhelmed by a new sense of what the poem means:

> *"Think of your breed; for brutish ignorance*
> *Your mettle was not made; you were made men,*
> *To follow after knowledge and excellence."*

As if I also was hearing it for the first time: like the blast of a trumpet, like the voice of God. For a moment I forget who I am and where I am.

Pikolo begs me to repeat it. How good Pikolo is, he is aware that it is doing me good. Or perhaps it is something more: perhaps, despite the wan translation and the pedestrian, rushed commentary, he has received the message, he has felt that it has to do with him, that it has to do with all men who toil, and with us in particular; and that it has to do with us two, who dare to reason of these things with the poles for the soup on our shoulders.

I don't think the world of AIDS can be fairly compared to the world of concentration camps. Even if it could, I'm not a prisoner; so it may be presumptuous of me to feel the kinship with the clients that Levi does with his fellow-prisoner in this passage. What does correspond, though, is the unexpected power of the text. As Levi struggles to recall, translate, and explain Dante to his companion, the poem—or Levi's generous enthusiasm—works its magic: perhaps for Levi alone (the text is very honest on this point), perhaps for them both.

My initial misgivings to the contrary, the essential contradiction isn't between compassion and truthtelling. To soothe and to point out are both gestures, and the real choice is whether or not to make any gesture at all. Somehow (I realized this after reading the Levi) the choice has been made for me; I hardly feel I've made it myself. Two of the men I worked with have died; more will die. The shuffle and disorder of sheaves of unfinished poems, signifying so many incomplete acts and decisions in a truncated life, make their writers as present to me as plenty of people I see many times a week. In September I hope to go back to the loft where "all the conventions conspire/To make this fort assume/The furniture of home" (though rumor has it that GMHC has bought a building and we'll have spiffy new quarters, the furniture of home will probably be the same) and once there I'll try to help poetry make nothing happen again—and again and again.

II

AIDS AND THE ART OF LIVING

AIDS *and the* Art *of* Living

THIS SECTION consists of forty-five poems and prose poems by Charles Barber, Glenn Besco, Dan Conner, Tony J. Giordano, Kevin Imbusch, Glenn Philip Kramer, Raul Martinez-Avila, and James Turcotte.

A few of these pieces—two of Glenn Kramer's contributions and some of the Conner and Turcotte poems—are earlier work brought to and perhaps revised in the workshop at GMHC. With the exception of poems written in the hospital, the rest of the work gathered here was written in the context of the workshop between the fall of 1989 and early 1991.

The provenance of some poems is obvious: Wallace Stevens's "Thirteen Ways of Looking at a Blackbird" and "Domination of Black" signal their presence in three titles. Other titles ("Ghazals a Go-Go," "Pantoum for Dark Mornings," "Letter Poem," "Prose Poem," "Fall Sonnets") also hint clearly at particular assignments. Often, though, assignments disappeared into the work they occasioned: "Room 3366, Bed 1" answered a call for a poem in dialogue, but left the assignment far behind. Perhaps "Vernon Weidner Visits" and "Lapel Button" incorporate dream material in response to another assignment; I no longer remember.

The point is that it doesn't matter. Any specific assignment can be thought of as a challenge, a nudge, a *point d'appui*, a hurdle. What matters is how consistently the poems that came in week by week transcended the immediate occasions of their composition. Inevitably, each poem reflected its writer's particular style, mood, experience, dream, and so on; yet this very fidelity seemed to enable many of the poems to reach beyond individuality. In other words, art was working its magic.

When it was time to pick out and arrange the strongest work for this book, I wasn't surprised to find the poems entering into dialogue with one another. Seasons or visits, hospitalizations or memories—the separate poems corroborate or revise what their neighbors have to say. Of course the conversation is somewhat discontinuous; the movement from one poem to another can be bumpy, forcing the reader to negotiate gaps. Yet these gaps, these spaces, these silences were always part of the psychic terrain, the emotional weather, of the afternoons at the workshop. Mikhail Bakhtin writes:

> Life in language is . . . dependent upon the preservation of a gap.
> Two speakers must not, and never do, completely understand each

other; they must remain only partially satisfied with each other's replies, because the continuation of dialogue is in large part dependent on neither party knowing exactly what the other means. Thus true communication never makes languages sound the same, never erases boundaries, never pretends to a perfect fit.

In presenting these voices, I keep thinking of two images, both of which seem to approach the central meaning of what was happening in the workshop. In one of his letters to a young poet, Rilke calls love and death "two problems that we carry wrapped up and hand on without opening." And Kenneth Burke defines life as an "unending dialogue: when we enter, it's already going on; we try to get the drift of it; we leave before it's over."

The dialogue in the workshop was and is unending—so much so that to extract these forty-five poems gives a misleading sense of finality, as if a canon were being closed. Precisely because "we leave before it's over," no one participant in the dialogue is in a position to answer the question—to unwrap the shared problem—posed in the penultimate poem here, Kramer's "What Happens." At the same time, by asking this and other questions over and over in their several voices—by passing the unwrapped problem around the table—the following poems do fashion a kind of answer.

AIDS and the Art of Living

All this breaks down to a mental
state. For the record. I'm afraid
sometimes to leave this studio.
Everything's art, everything is
if you see it that way. Dying's
no different, living as always
the same issue: breath and
breakfast, *"What do you want?"*
What is it you want to do
to fill time, what do you
need? We look to the cosmos
and see the dishes in our sink.
I'm afraid to leave this efficiency
for fear I'll crap my pants: what
American doesn't share in this
same fear: bodily functions
on the crosstown bus, something
taboo at the banquet, incontinent,
incapable, potentially senile, dying
of embarrassment? We'll leave this
party all together,
        confident someone
else will clean up. Confidence
left me on the operating table.
Our issue from birth is confidence: how
you will sleep in the night, turning
again to dawn, arising, stretching
blood out to the finger tips. These
are the hands with which I write, make
notes, once again I feed myself today.

Dan Conner

Thirteen Things About A Catheter

White tube
In cephalic vein;
To the right atrium
Of the heart (see illustration):
Access.

A cuff,
Made of dacron,
Serves as a barrier
To infections, tunneled under
The skin.

Daily
I tend its bud,
Swabbing away the dust,
The slugs of dirt that in the night
Advance.

The nurse
Is called Bud, too:
A gay man, but grumpy;
Won't use my towels, asks "don't you have. . .
Paper?"

A fish,
Hung from the pole,
Striped with words of caution:
"To expire in ninety-one"
(Like me?)

The bag,
Bloated with drug,
Takes the hook at line's end;
Hopeful and still, I reel it in,
Dripping . . .

Detached,
Or pulled apart,
Silently blood spurts out;
I stare at it uncaringly,
Unmoved.

Or sex:
A white t-shirt
Discreetly veils the thing.
Between us, while locked together,
It hurts.

Bandaged,
Walking wounded,
The cap beneath my shirt
Signals to other veterans:
"Soldier."

A kite,
Flapping skyward,
Dreaming only of the ground,
While dirty hands keep the string tight,
Tired.

Or Mom
With aging son,
Feeds from her third nipple,
Thinks: "Please won't you go away soon,
Dear one."

The dream.
Finally well,
Over me lies his arm;
The hole in my chest a lip-smudge,
Stamped, sealed.

Grotesque,
Life-supporting,
Deforming and healing;
Not a cure; insistent I be
Life-like.

            Charles Barber

Isolation

they wouldn't bring me the food
the tray was left outside
my room because they were
afraid to come in, afraid
of catching god knows what.
the tray remained where it was
until a masked nurse had the
kindness to bring it into the
room and finally uncover
what was once food.

eyes, eyes nothing but eyes
faces hidden behind blue masks
sometimes i was frightened
frightened of: eyes detached
from nose, from mouth; words
seemed to come from nowhere,
to say nothing.

i told most everyone to stay
away, not to visit. had to sleep.
lulled by the endless silence.
bed-bound. not able to move from
the prison bed, the lovely soft
bed, the island bed, the hated bed.

high fevers and sleep. dreams
and hallucinations riveting me
to bed, to pillow. what was
said was real yet a dream.
why was i frightened all the time?

night sweats. clammy wet sheets
peeled off of skin like the peeling
of an orange. in the dark, in the
cold wet dark, in the cold silence
and aloneness i lie. then the chills.
the unrelenting shaking of my
body, the chattering of teeth like
a pair of castanets. the sweat and
chill mixed. the arrival of nurse and

then into warm things, into warm dry things.
and sleep.
the nightmare journey continues
alone.

Tony J. Giordano

Room 3366, Bed 1

I'm your new partner, Bed.
Sure glad you were empty.
More comfy than the ER gurney.
Seems we were almost wed.

Glad to meet you, guy.
Wiggle around a tad.
Last guy laid so still, so sad.
Massage me with your thigh.

That guy did he meet his doom?
I hope you were not a deadman's bed.
Tell me he went home instead.
Or transferred to another room.

People go and come. That gent
Transferred to the slab.
Never even took him to the lab.
Some go home, others to the basement.

Bed, let's change our view.
I was wondering. So . . .
Did a patient—ever—you know?
Anyone ever get on on you?

Death and Sex same questions again.
Other things can happen.
Stay with me I can make you a man.
You upset, I'm not a virgin?

No, it was a relief to slide over on you.
You were sanitized, deodorized,
Prophylactized and exorcised.
I like this spot. It will do.

You flatter me when you speak.
I am already your friend.
Together to the end.
Neither of us sad or meek.

Is dying like an orgasm?
Do you know when it will come?
Which illness will be the one?
Bed, I'm terrified of the chasm!

You're not dying now. Take ease.
But you will do it alone.
All I can do is be along.
Rest, my friend. Be at peace.

Glenn Besco

People Come Out of the Woodwork

Now I can eat all the desserts I want. Now I am free to speak my mind. Now I have time to write my thoughts. I can watch Bewitched or Wheel of Fortune any day. Now I have plenty of time on my hands. I have retired. I am a student again. I get to go to movies. And to plays. Now I share in the true spirit of my friends.

Doctors are human. Doctors are businessmen. Doctors are witchdoctors. Doctors are the hands of God. Doctors can kill. Sometimes doctors can offer miracles to those who ask. Sometimes not.

Hospitals are not hotels. Hospitals are like the subway: filled with strangers who might harm you, no privacy. Hospitals are places of business. Hospitals are not a place to sleep. Some hospitals are good, some bad. Hospitals are in the eye of the beholder.

Nurses wake people up. Nurses must wake people to make them swallow things. Nurses must wake people to take their temperatures. Nurses must wake people to weigh them. And to clean their rooms at 4:00 A.M. Nurses are overworked. Some nurses have the healing touch. Some don't.

If I sleep too much I will never get up. If I do too much I will fall down, fall down and go to the hospital. Once I fell down and didn't get up for ten weeks. I was given a nurse to take home. She liked my cats. She didn't like muggers. I had a cat who ran away. She mourned my cat she never knew. Cats are worth saving. Muggers are not. For muggers she kept a can of roach spray in her purse. If they got her wallet they'd also get a shot in the eyes. Blinds them temporarily.

Hospital food is not all bad. Hospital food saved my life. Chicken. Chicken is a great source of protein. The kitchen gave me chicken for any lunch or dinner I wanted. Except when they were out. Then I got a cheese sandwich.

Walking is important. Everyday, down corridors, with the I.V., pole and pump. My rod and staff, they comfort me. Hospitals are not art galleries, but they try to be. Hospital corridors don't have stairs. Or wind. Walking put me back on my feet.

TPN is expensive. Interferon is expensive. AZT is expensive. Home care is expensive. Looking at bills would make you crazy if it weren't so ludicrous. I never look at the bills. Someone else will pay them.

Some brave people are scared of hospitals. Some get nightmares, daymares from tiled floors and walking ghosts. They will not come, but they will call. They will not call if you want to talk shop. Some bring flowers, strained smiles, balloons. Some fall asleep. Some will not touch you. Some look out the window.

Some will sit and talk, will sit and listen, will let the nurses' station know what is wrong, will massage your feet. Some patients have friends who climb into bed with them, hold them like babes, stroke away the fears.

Some brave people who are scared of hospitals are patients. They will do anything, anything to avoid going in. Hospitals can make you sick. Hospitals are where people go to die. A hospital stay saved my life.

Some patients are good. They do what the good doctors say. Some patients are too good, drifting into some overworked doctor's silent failure.

Some patients are bad. They rant and rave and throw fits all hours in loud voices about the food and their lack of pain killers and unanswered bells and unshut doors and the noise in the hall, keeping everyone else awake and disturbed. And some smoke in their rooms and throw away their pills and try to go to the lobby in their bathrobe and sandals and some won't eat and some steal food and some steal liquor and some smoke grass and some steal watches and books and jewelry and clothes and constantly try to bum cigarettes off the same people who never smoke. Some hoard their methadone. Some have friends bring in speed or coke or crack or horse.

The best patients know which medicines are theirs and which aren't. They know when to make a ruckus. They ask too many questions. They never take a test without knowing why.

The best patients also know the value of the words "thank you." Sometimes fighting isn't enough.

I believe in a long life. I believe in the potential for a long life. I desire to live a long life. I know I can live a long time. I know I can live to be seventy. I will sit in a rocker and look back on my years of hardship, of hardship and pleasure.

My faith is my recovery. My faith is the source of my recovery. My recovery is the origin of my faith. I am my own testimonial. I believe others will help me. I believe others will help me because others have helped me. Life will not be easy. If I can't handle it, others will. I like handling it, when I can. I do my paperwork. Some days I don't. I will need the help of others. People come out of the woodwork. People come to help out. The help we share is the love that will save us.

Dan Conner

29

Ghazal: The Quick and The Dead

Who has, with most temerity, scaled the heights, the quick or the
dead?
The one, alive in pain, the other, at rest, but gone: condemned to
   blights
                              are the quick and the dead.

Do the quick, with courage, struggle for self-forgetfulness,
While the dead recall, recall? Long are the tossing nights
                        of the quick and the dead.

Can life, lived, out-stretch death, achieved?
The present moment offers tasks, as well as flights,
                           to the quick and the dead.

And which lays claim to perpetuity?
Both can speak of ever-lastingness; widely range the sights
                         of the quick and the dead.

But after all, the quick survive; the dead are doornails.
Down hospital hallways are heard the lingering fights
                         between the quick and the
                                                 dead.

Work hard, cries one; give in, the other;
Each a difficult path of endless plights
                      for the quick and the dead.

Some move between the two; now quick, now dead,
Then quick again. Off and on in the rooms go the lights
                        of the quick and the dead.

Live or die, the lights seem to say, blinking in silence.
Ponderings of this most final question are the chief delights
                         of the quick and the dead.

Charles Barber

A Teddy Bear

A Teddy Bear just sits and looks.
The Teddy Bear's arms and legs may move.
He has no control over where they are put
Or the position in which he is left for another day.

A Teddy Bear's eyes look out at the faces
Of the people in the room.
He knows their secrets,
He knows their joys and gloom.
He knows he exists to be the one who
Receives the terror of a two year old
The abuse of big brother or sister
The love of a lonely adult.

A Teddy likes to be squeezed and tugged and pulled.
It is like a massage from a powerful masseuse.
Even being dragged by his heels can be all right.
At least it gives a new point of view.
Most of all the Teddy likes to be held and hugged and loved.
A Teddy is just here.
He never complains or catches a virus.

He especially likes the adult people who admit
That in his furry warmth they find comfort.
He likes the warmth of a fevered body
With arms clutched around him.
He likes the times when he is alone with an adult.
They talk together of times past and times to come.
They pour out today's bitches.

A Teddy Bear exists to give love, joy and peace.
He exists until all has been given and received.
Teddy knows everything.
He listens when no one imagines he hears.
He knows all the latest tests,
All the experimental drugs and their side effects.
He knows that the arms that hold him may soon go cold and hard.
He knows all the secrets of the night nurses.

Glenn Besco

The Storm

the storm outside battering
battering against the glass
steamy radiators
now cold, silent, dead
an icy stream of darkness
drowns all comfort

beneath mounds of sheets,
quilts and blankets
shivering, shivering
burrowing deep within
a region of short shaky breaths
eyes peering through a
chink in the thick fabric wall
illuminated digits
blink in the darkness:

9am   3am
    8am   4am
        7am   5am
            6am

Tony J. Giordano

Pantoum for Dark Mornings

It's all just dumb show, anyway.
Our dreams, our getting through the day.
There's nothing on the scales to weigh.
My life's become a shadow play.

Our dreams, our getting through the day.
I keep alive by pills which beep.
My life's become a shadow play.
I want to do no more than sleep.

I keep alive by pills which beep.
A friend, he says I'm going to die.
I want to do no more than sleep.
My stupor sometimes lets me cry.

A friend, he says I'm going to die.
A foe, of course, in friend's disguise.
My stupor sometimes lets me cry.
But mostly I just close my eyes.

A foe, of course, in friend's disguise.
My sense of judgment spurts out blood.
But mostly I just close my eyes.
And lie here waiting for the flood.

My sense of judgment spurts out blood.
I want to die most every day.
And lie here waiting for the flood.
It's all just dumb show, anyway.

Glenn Philip Kramer

Domination of Black

This night, while the cold
wind pounds glass, the white
walls, all four framing
silence, the ear, our inner ear,
echoes the hollow peacocks' cry,
demanding and frightened, echoes
still, and the hemlocks wait.

> All our proud peacocks!
> The colors of their tails
> were the leaves and
> more turning; the colors
> gold, a royal lavender;
> the textured satin
> glistening, fanned out;
> dancing, preening,
> prancing the promenade.
> In the urban twilight
> stars swept the floor.

> I witnessed how the planets
> converged: Hercules, Atlas,
> Neptune in a sea of light.
> Peacocks swept over the room
> just as the leaves flew
> from the lofty boughs
> of hemlocks, hemlocks behind them.

> They flew, they flew turning
> down to the ground.

> I heard them cry—the peacocks
> turned against the dawn
> for a chance to dream.

We turn in a loud fire, turn
in a wind grown loud, louder
than the empty hemlocks.
> Were they
crying against the twilight, or
did they greet the brittle dawning?
Could they bear what that closing light

betrayed? Was it all so much feathery
leaves fallen fast to the cold earth
that made the peacocks sing the night's
end? And who now craves the hemlock?

For now the wind gathers
full force: the storm.
Brown leaves rake the pane,
withered and scraped up, tethered
to this westerly. The cry,
turned full rattles the glass.
The bitter wind tears it sharp
from the throat. Their cry
is my anger. Out of my window
I watch night fall again
        and again there is no time
for hemlocks now. I will not fear,
cannot, but walk full force
        out into the wind, the cold —
walk out, beyond the dark. I bear
no fear, for I have held them crying.

Dan Conner

Fall Sonnets

1

Trying to reason, trying to rhyme,
to craft myself in pleasant conversation,
I think a lot about the time
I've got. My situation.

Projected as the image of my friends
in hospitals (in prison),
today collapses into bed, is a handful of attendants
offering control as substance, with injections.

No personal appliances, no laptops here.
Deluxe is sheets and soap, not having to explain.
Nothing but a pen and paper,
and remember, Don't complain.

The currency of bloodwork is,
Think Positive.

2

The park is like a tapestry.
Yellow, deepened with illusions,
black boughs, a scrim of leaves in dusty green
the summer flutters through.

Leaf by leaf, a hint of red, of clay,
of rust, motion is a sea of trees,
each with its tale of happier days—
Remember me!

So now I've got this picture.
I've got to get my words to play,
(science meeting art at form and structure),
remake myself as valuables you put away.

For death is the turn where scene and science part.
The point of art was never really truth, but art.

James Turcotte

I Sat Through a Distant Autumn

i sat through a distant autumn
watching trees grow old and shed
their gold and brown crisp leaves
i sat by a window looking down
at traffic and people rushing
to their destinations
unaware that i sat watching them
and envying them their lives
of purpose and mobility
while i sat like an invalid
waiting out time
looking at a brilliant landscape
the village rooftops
quaint, safe, charming
the towering twin towers
gleaming in the sun
i sat through a distant autumn
watching the magnificence
of flying birds and planes
of freedom in all forms
i marveled at the energy
the movement
the vitality
so much i lacked
and wished for
and feared i could never have again
i sat through a distant autumn
unsure of spring

Tony J. Giordano

Bar Light

Holding on to health and youth
denies the madness that's eternity.
What matter, keeping light
from passing through the chink in duty
could mean more than this—
the bar and hopeless dreaming, smoke and mirrors—
that we live for?

What tour of duty could reveal the vanity
of promises more swift and more appealing
than a derelict kiss, or flash of vision
from tomorrow's distant laughter?

Too soon the music disappears.
Mistrust's stalagmites brought to light
forget the sweet breath of musician's chords.
Don't talk to me about eternity, for

evening's magnetic mirrors,
a slowdown in the mind of hopeful drifters,
capture softness moving gentle wishes
over notes of weekend pulses.

Did you know this? That all the stage
is just creation entertaining us?
That breath is all we need?

James Turcotte

Sunday March

I imagine the March as vividly as if I were there.
Lying in the hospital bed—
Drowsy, suspended in a cloud of half-dreams
A cast of characters tumble in and out
Like a cast of lunatics in an eight-door bedroom farce—
And I smile, almost giggle, nearly cry.
The bright piercing truth of day
Gusts merrily through the window screen
And sirens, the city's soprano voice,
Sing arias of danger, emergency, now, quick, life.
Balloons, banners, bands—everything in a
March
Everything in my life,
My life of quiet glory—
I march alone, I march with thousands.
I know those eyes of happy wonder
Seeing only the bright colors of silky dusk.
Waving, waving never wavering.
Embraces of an acrobatic love flying with ease.
I dream a drowsy dream of you,
Your hard hairy chest crushing mine.
Our parade is a long ritual
And if time takes our side
The March continues.

Tony J. Giordano

The Obsidian Mountain

When I was young my Mom and Dad
used to drive me down to the old rock shop
on the edge of town, full of dust of clay
and the smell of oil from the grinding wheels
that shrieked against the stones.

There were gems and crystals, agates
and minerals of every color and texture;
and, in a little box by the cash register,
volcanic glass, tear drops a nickel apiece,
tears from the heart of fire.

Clear, or translucent and tinted by ash,
some black as midnight, glimmering ovals
tumbling through my fingers, smooth to touch.
Permanent tears, tears in my pocket,
tears that transport light.

Now I stand on a summit of tears,
tears from my heart, on fire, tears
that transport light from within. I stand
and watch the evening approach
quietly out of the east.

I stand on this Obsidian Mountain
and peer down through to the heart of the world,
down through rippled waters of stone
descending under my feet. Oh, how my heart
ascends to the awakening stars.

Dan Conner

Flying to Ireland

Suddenly, there it is—
like green slime
on the ocean's dawn-lit face,
waving her sea-wrack tresses,
welcoming.
Can this be my native land
this strange mass?

From long absence
she is a stranger to me now
and yet she weaves spells
embracing the whole world for me.

We descend down, down, down
into her damp grassy bosom,
and touch.
She has spread an emerald carpet under my feet.

I want to fall on my knees and kiss her
(like some wandering Pope)
but I just walk gently
knowing I'm home.

Kevin Imbusch

Tornado Touch Down at Worth, Mo.

Granny Maxwell sits alone on her porch.
Lot's wife, she must see the power of divine wrath.
She sits as silent as the moments before the holocaust.
Boiled, cracked chicken heads left from her meal lay
beside her, beneath the concern of darkness. She grips
the pillow in her wheelchair.
This time she is immune from death.

All nature sounds stop. Air, water and earth
creatures all stand still. Sudden silence. Sounds cease.
Birds hang in flight. Flowers give up their scent.

The green-gray cloud boils low over housetops.
It paints the sheds a chilling greenish color.
The white light is compressed to the ground by the
piercing funnel.

Bessie looks up. Her cud caught in her throat.
Her milk curdles in her udder.

From pole to pole dark forces converge. The confluence
will suck into infinity this place of memories.

The Methodist Church steeple ascends from the roof,
elevated in space before it completes its
transformation into junk.

Hens in the yard are plucked and delivered head first
into wire fences ten miles away.

A ten-foot 2 x 4 hurls into orbit. The crazy
force rams it forward through the wall into the
flour bin in Betty's kitchen cabinet.

Granny Myers is carried into the cellar outside the hotel.
A dozen or more people clutch at each other. The cave smells of
rotten potatoes and stale water. The cobwebs dangle in their faces.
Granny had forgotten to save her teeth.

The man next to Granny Myers is gone. He had released his hold
to scratch his nose.

Glenn Besco

Lost Monday

lost life lost
agony in unspoken words
debtor to a dying breed
monster with savage eyes
stalks within
echoes of a time
buried deep within my life
resound faintly
as now, in this devastating
silence
as now, suspended in
solitude
why is happiness never
speaking to Kevin
or is there ever happiness
speaking to anyone
his voice is high voltage
i mustn't touch!

Tony J. Giordano

What Was Said

Love said,
The garden is coolest   in the morning
See where the deer have not eaten   the stone lion speaks

Dismay said,
How has this happened   to me   what did I do   where has it come
    from
        go away

Illness said,
Now you will wait beyond all suffering   suffer beyond all knowing
Small moments   will not exist   only the large hand unfolding and
    folding

Childhood said,
The cars   the Tonka Toy cars   they carry me small as Stuart Little
        home over the hill

The table by the window said,
The lamp   the lake   the bowl of peonies   the pad and pen
        Now evening comes

Remorse said,
It was the golden ball   hanging over the pool table   shimmering
    beckoning
        turning slow as futility

Hopefulness said,
Red will be there   the red-curtained theatre   the plate of red beets
        the red-faced mailman at noon

The friend said,
Meanings collapse   we go along   variously lost   dinner done
        repeating stories

Old age said,
I kick   I cry   put down the cup   find in the basement parking lot
        the car marked "rest"

Dying, I said,
I am the preyed upon   I stand in line   shuffling   uneasy   marked
        the sun   a disappointment   small   pale
        locating no one as it arches into airlessness.

    Charles Barber

44

Wars

1

A dark cloud hangs over the countryside, everyone asking,
What is it?

Its message is penumbral, a quarantine on country boys, a
logic spelling war on unusual moves. Blinded by a
supernatural love for goddesses, young oracles pose as
outlaws in the wilderness, defending mass communication.
Blood is drawn, bearing the tragicomic mask of
confrontation.

This cloud has set the son against his father's house.

2

The secrets of war—a love willing to die for—music and
media conspire to seal a kiss with pictured victory in
another land.

The words, I love you, spoken in the youthful voices of the
stars, and music, masterful as a modern symphony in
imageland's perpetual moment, emerge as drama and release.
Memory flies in space ships, off to save another day.

Manufacturers and syndicators sit with private hesitations,
watching product—research's timebomb—sink quietly into
orbit.

When this night is over, who will wear the crown?

3

The black hole of media eats luxuries—truth, and
fact—releasing voyeuristic journeys that project in time,
like light years guided at tomorrow's vision of collapsing
stars.

Saxophone and rhythm sections back up singers in a moment's
madness, smooth as a note or two. A junket. Fluid passion
in a night that ain't that long. A stoned soul picnic,
distant trumpets drifting through a summer window, death is
calling in a warming wind of satisfaction.

Do it any way you want it, do it any way you want. Records remember, keep in store emotion's undercurrent, but can't be played these days. We listen through the scratches, read between the lines.

Souls without bodies, we live in time. Pressed in vinyl. Life's discography.

James Turcotte

Maturity

There is never enough time to become a man.
Somewhere we get stuck like eggs in a pan.
We sit and soak, we wait to move on.
We want to loosen but all our chances are gone.

I say "I am a man." I say, "I'm strong!"
But what does it mean, why am I wrong?
Maturity, that's the goal. By what standard?
Who is to judge, who says, "Missed by a yard!"?

Sometimes we are pushed suddenly to decide.
No time to linger, no time to hide.
All our future is shaped in a moment.
No time to tarry, no time to lament.

I do a man's work, I pull a man's load.
Inside I feel like a newcomer to the road.
There is a conflict. I am torn between
What I know I am and what others have seen.

Glenn Besco

A Maze of Decades

am i there with the strawberry vanilla oozing down my face
looking up with cunning green eyes wanting more and more and
getting it—maybe

am i there with the dark brown suit fitting a bit too tight
and the shirt collar and bright yellow tie taut around my
neck

am i there standing at the coffin looking at a face that seems
familiar and yet that pasty waxy half-smile was not put there by
God, oh no

am i there running and out of breath, frightened, desperate, my
ears pricked at every sound, and that one sound in particular: a
bully's footstep

am i there holding you in my arms taking in the smell of
cologne and sweat, feeling the warmth of your nicotined breath on
my face

am i there walking down Lexington Avenue while the pain is
shooting across my chest, down through my arm, feeling nauseous
and frightened and dizzy, dizzy from the teeming rush hour crowds

am i there crawling on my belly, buttons popping and my pants
slithering down my groin and legs as the bullets whiz overhead
in a dry run at Ft. Dix

am i there standing in the darkness, in the long narrow closet
where the smell of wool and lint and moth balls stifles my breath,
waiting for Sister Miriam Agnes to let me out

am i there in that not too cheerful hallway carrying the last
carton of books and closing the door to my new apartment, living
away from home for the first time

am i there preparing for a surprise birthday party for you which
you know all about because of your insistence that we have dinner
together

am i there seated snugly in front of you in the last
car of the Cyclone at Coney Island, slowly, slowly
ever slowly, going up that first hill with your erection

am i there seated across the table from you with my cup of
coffee and the scrambled eggs, dodging all your questions
and trying not to look in your eyes

am i there sitting by your bed at the hospital and praying
as i never prayed before that some miracle would happen
and you would come out of the coma

am i there sleeping with someone whose name i can't remember
while you wait in agony for my return, only to listen to my
shabby stumbling lies

am i there lying in the e.r. at St. V's with you looking at
me with frightened eyes and wanting to know and not wanting to
know and me telling you everything and nothing at all

am i there as the lights come up on that dingy space on
E. 2nd Street, as the actors begin to speak the words i've
written

Tony J. Giordano

Ghazals a Go-Go

Bright purple teeth bopped to the music, hinting of sex.
The world was a-go-go in the sixties.

We took orange sunshine and tripped off to movies
Trying to help Dorothy find her Toto in the sixties.

CIVIL RIGHTS! straight boys shouted on campuses.
But women and gays were still a no-no in the sixties.

Hitchhiking defiantly on brittle cold roads
I secretly wished Donna Reed would bring cocoa, in the sixties.

Men were walking on the moon; I'd try overdosing soon.
My mental health was so-so in the sixties.

After Zeffirelli's R&J, I searched the first time for a man,
Scared but proud to be a homo in the sixties.

Glenn Philip Kramer

Prose Poem

But no, the palm trees had no reply. Clifford searched the beach, of course a sea of garbage. A real anachronism, a sweatshirt in Florida: still, babies huddled by the outdoor pool, scarily close to the golfcourse, upending their blue drinks or squeezing into the hot-tub. At night, the family pushed little letters around the Scrabble board, sending each other furtive messages disguised as simple squares, emotional Chiclets. The sky yielded not one inch though he begged for its friendship. Here and there carts darted among the bushes. Oldsters laughed, was it "gaily"? Security was tight. The project to chase down some herons for their sperm to make AZT came to naught when a dispatch in the form of the Times informed them it was herrings, not herons, that they should be seducing. Where, oh where, are there herrings on a golfcourse? Mary preferred flamingoes anyway she said. Everywhere, too much food. Bicycling in the Ding Darling Bird Preserve cleared their heads, until numerous alligators stared challengingly. "Mom, Mom," he cried out, but it was the Gulf Coast. Land mines would have helped. Strangely, the landscape was void of teens, all the skins wrinkled or new; perhaps a terrible blight? Cliff would have to search for the teens. There are teens on golfcourses, a childhood lesson learned hard and fast. But pleasure had made him languid, a kind of sunny poison. There was no hardship. Still, the house shook on the moorings. Still, the Scrabble letters slid dangerously this way and that. Still, the rain fell.

Charles Barber

Thirteen Ways to Look at a Son

I
Often I dream of you, young—
        riding on my shoulders—going fishing.
Do you ever dream of being a boy?

II
Branch growing from the root of the family.
        Branch on branch reaching far for freedom,
Dying without the lifegiving blood of the root.

III
I want to hold you as we sink
        Into a warm goo of memories.
You are like the tar fly never sinking.

IV
Warm hugger, tolerant, silent.
        You stood by as I left you.
All the while my guilt wept at our separation.

V
Near and far is real.
        Warm embracing Hellos.
Tears and Goodbyes.
        Our wordless talks in between.

VI
Stud-like self assurance,
        Narcissus re-incarnate.
I join the people ready to worship you.

VII
You are like a cat.
        Proud, independent—
with your incessant soft purring demands.

VIII
Heart far bigger than head!
        Your hands give without care for self.
Often you are the used one left behind.

IX
Impetuous!
        Your actions tumble over themselves—
Energy released like a bursting mountain waterfall.

X
Potential building to eruption—
        As uncontrolled as your hard rock guitar.
Talent you toy with, bat around like a cat's ball.

XI
Clark Kent, Strong Defender of
        Truth, Justice and the American Way.
Not a cliché. Not really a Superboy.

XII
An image on a wall,
        a shadow, a silhouette.
Which is you and which is me?

XIII
Seed of my loins, genes of my genes.
        I proudly set you free
                TO BE . . .

Glenn Besco

Letter Poem

Dear Future,

What a tease you are, big old gassy thing,
Up there on the stage week in and week out;
In something pink and overdone you sing
While down below hoary customers shout.
How the floorboards squeak as you prance about,
Flushed, professional, critics at your feet.
What a life it is to shimmy and flout,
A feather boa where neck and chin meet.
I saw your show once when I was on the beat,
You sang: "Fortune's always hiding, I've looked
Everywhere": how bad the sound from my seat!
But by an old stagey charm I was hooked:
Nightly, past the light of the big cigar
In the box office, come to where you are.

Dear Present Moment,

Never to be described, but fully lived,
You're a slow summer evening, not yet dark,
The sighs of lengthening shadows vivid
In the withdrawing sky and distant park.
The train from the city a modern ark:
We left newspapers scattered on the floor.
Now against the sight of sprinkler and bark,
Gathered on the terrace by the french door,
Ignoring piled-up dishes and more,
We count the fireflies that haunt the dusk,
Each a bright allegiance we happily swore,
Tonight we breathe the scent of earth and musk,
Creep down with flashlights leading our pleasure
To see the night-blooming cereus together.

Dear Memory,

Last night, from my window, there I saw you,
Passing along the dark narrow sidewalk.
It was late but not so late that a few
Stragglers weren't still winding home deep in talk.
Some of them I noticed seemed to gawk

At you, and stare; some averted their gaze.
How sad you looked, thin, and eyes like a hawk—,
Slumped over, pushing that cart, lost in a maze.
Too many coats, proudly worn, set in your ways.
Not enough in the way of shoes, or hat
To shield you from the cold or cloudy haze
Of the moon as it picks out fence and rat.
"So my past is homeless now too," I thought,
And slammed the window on the glimpse I'd caught.

Charles Barber

Saturday Night

Do I resent the sounds of furious living?
From my hospital room window is heard
The cacophony of Saturday night noises;
      from within is the flood of darkness.
I drown in a whirlpool
Of imagination.
Everyone speeding, spinning;
The roar of Saturday night living goes on.

While thick in the silence of these hospital walls
Down, down somewhere down the hall
Explodes the agony
Of one individual retching up his guts
While the quick patter of nurse's footsteps
comes and goes in aid.

I listen to the sounds of furious living
      within and without.

Tony J. Giordano

Vernon Weidner Visits in a Dream

It's moving time.
Confusion reigns, boxes, boxes, furniture askew.
Who's moving? Where are they going?
Why this confusion—moving—changing—
beginning again—grasping—reaching?
Why am I alone? Doesn't anyone care?
A Momentum Board meeting at this house! Here! Now!
I'll be right there!

Vernon Weidner is not on the board.
Vern and Jean at my house. Jean will see my secret.
Vern knows I have AIDS.
Someone dropped a tray of glasses!
Why is he here? Vernon is a gentleman.
Vern has hurt his finger. His "bird" is swollen and taped.
His production is short of his goals—not on top this year.
How can he always be number one?
We discuss the business—my health—his health.
I ask about other agents. He smiles.
There are things he doesn't talk about.
Email—LB Link, Log on, modem—a new language—
new tools—new technology.
How could I ever go back to work with that?
Vernon understands. An old gentleman.
Aggressive salesman. Set in his ways. Grits his teeth.
Always able to change.
He knows the score.

Suddenly Vern Weidner appeared in my dream.
Part of the chaos or part of the calm?
Bringing answers or questions?
To goad me or support me?
At year's end to measure my work?

Why did he come when I was not settled?
Why did he come when the Momentum Board was meeting?

Glenn Besco

The Meal

this has nothing to do with eating
but with the dinner plate
and where it's placed on the table
and the layout of that table
and the people who dine at that table
she to my left
he to my right
i sit across from the tv
the living color news,
jeopardy, vanna white are there
in all their gory might
a snug dinner for four

this has nothing to do with food
although it's piled high on the plate
this has to do with him plowing
through the meal
sipping, gulping a glass or two of scotch
and running to the bathroom
throwing it all up

this has nothing to do with cooking
but the aching slow dance of aging
and the creaking of bones
and the shattered dreams
crashing like plates and glasses
in the steamy kitchen

this has nothing with do with dessert
she complaining about the puerto
ricans next door or the blacks
or the jews or my aunt upstairs
she giving updates of the family news
while the tv supplies us a good healthy
dose of robberies, murders, rapes
and Georgie Bush and coca cola commercials

this has nothing to do with tasting
it has to do with swallowing words
words of frustration and anger
each of us caught in a crossfire

of pointedly pointless conversation
i channeling my anger through politics
or anecdotes or rhetoric
he reminiscing about when he
was young and did this
and when he was young and did that
and how the world is not quite
the world it used to be
she eating cookies

this has nothing to do with dining
but living in a tight space
and loving as best one can
this is tv seven nights a week
this is a wrestling match
this is america's saturday night date
this is prime time
this is me on the F train
heading back to Manhattan

Tony J. Giordano

Little Family

My son and I ride bikes
down floodless concrete rivers
to the beach. Power plants
and sentinels of oil stand clear
of our sublime and silent run.

Bright rims turn under open skies,
past flowers in the desert vista.
Like a pair of racers with a torch,
we pursue another hour
of the world at large.

Around the bend's a distant bridge
where pelicans and herons splash—
more natural egotists at play.
A placid water gap and seagull runway
flicker in the winter sun.

Timid girls from school ride by. I wave
at names my son reveals. The small
embarrassed face reminds me he's thirteen
and Seal Beach twilight, turning amber,
tells him that it's time to eat.

We take each other's french fries
in reflections of two crazy weeks—
no family ever saw itself
like we do. You and me and grandma
having fun on our vacation,

not having to face facts,
never dreaming of tomorrow
till tonight. And now
it's over. Conviction's tears
are funny, looking back.

James Turcotte

Winter Memories

Days grow shorter in December.
Memories grow longer.
Jeb's fiery death and his family's agony.
Mom dead in her chair with dinner on the stove.
Too many cancer deaths in Hegewisch.
Marion and dozens of friends taken by AIDS.
Heart attacks and earthquakes.
My own deteriorating body.

Had I no past—
       I might fear the eternal winter
              fear the loss of hope
              fear the death of flowers
              fear my own death

God of light! Return!
The thinker tells me winter is but a cycle.
The feeler fears the worst has happened.
The prophet proclaims the promises of God.
I am all of them at once.

Glenn Besco

Inside His Borrowed Cage

Yes, planet Earth is immune suppressed
As it rotates on its prophylaxis.

I knew it would be.

The Prophets told me so,
Thousands of years ago.

Of course I am concerned.

But this poet has no rage
Inside his borrowed cage.

Instead, I choose to Believe.

I spend time with Angels
And in the unison
Of forgiving melodies,
Praise the Uncontained—
The Cageless
For creating the I in me,
For loving the I in me.

And so this poet travels
Each and every second of Time
Alongside Courage,
The journey to the Cageless
Of Crystal Clarity.
And how I resonate,
Oh, yes how I resonate,

For this poet has no rage
Inside his borrowed cage.

Raul E. Martinez-Avila

Retinitis

North vanishes as I turn east.

Vision is perforated, torn
along the line dotted
with floaters, galaxies
of gnats swimming.

This pebble dropped in
water of the eye
gives birth

to ripples in the sunlight glare.
Sometimes, in light so forced so bright
heads of friends aren't
on their necks, I raise my left hand
only to see it
vanish along

with Seventh Avenue and the blind rag

man, fat on his crutches
clutching the cup. Cobwebs,
networks of
light flashing
on new &
foreign shores.

At night, sometimes dim
except across that deepest
dark, lights that silhouette limbs of the most exotic
trees, lights burning on shores
that in broadest daylight
are not black,
not white,
not gray,
are
      not.
              Sometimes I reach into that manhole
of nothing dancing about my left shoulder,
out of the corner, that very corner
of this eye that first opened on the world
when I first surfaced: that eye, this

63

very corner, & the dancing manhole
of nothing I slip my hand in
it slips away, leaves my wrist
for foreign beaches only
and returns as untanned,
veined, milky white as ever. Square
and stumpy, nails bitten, life line still
unread, the hand I reel back in
to this Twentysecond streetglare.

Dan Conner

Lapel Button

A hot summer day.
I have slept too long,
once again,
and the air-conditioner
hanging over West 16th Street
streams.

I'd been watching a Callas video
of Alfred's,
to study the singer's clasped arms,
the constant dialogue
between actor and acted;
as Gordon once told me,
the sign of greatness
in a performer.

Hers is a private moment
that I am privileged to share;
"Let me reveal,"
says her pain,
"not only the thought,
but the thinker."
Somehow,
in this big stupid opera,
out of the darkness
of the wings,
and from behind the badly painted scenery
and fifties hair-do's,
there's suddenly a fusion
of sadness and knowledge.

Sleep . . .
Waking . . .
Confused by the all-white walls,
so like the ocean:
empty but everywhere.

I pull on my shorts,
shoes, my favorite plaid shirt
with the ripped shoulder from when

Laurent pulled it off David too fast,
stripping down in Paris.

In a flash of the elevator
I'm on Fifth Avenue,
long-legged, tan from the beach,
striding over poodles
and quite lost in self-love
and coffee smells.
Only my sneakers
on the pavement
hold me down.
The setting sun means:
ballet class, seltzer, endless time;
all of downtown
to be discovered,
the sun
pinned to my lapel,
a pink and orange
button of continuance.
                ***

Three years later,
and winter, oh boy
is it ever.
Adam and I eat Indian food
while he quizzes me
on my feelings for him,
which are less than they might be
if he was another someone.

We watch Rock Hudson
dying on T.V.
The actor playing
the actor
is not good, does not know
how to die.
Or at least, I wouldn't do it
that way;
he's not nearly tired enough;
his eyes are lively
the way they wouldn't be;
he blinks,

66

which requires too much strength
at that point;
his hair is tidy
and there is nothing caked on his face
except pancake;
he isn't gaunt enough; the bones
have not emerged thoughtfully
as they do when
knowledge
meets sadness
and it's just too late
in the afternoon.

That is the way
I would do it;
now I know,
but for all my being
a better actor
I will not do it,
anyway not on T.V.,
not for Equity minimum,
not in a swimsuit in Malibu,
not even clasped between Doris Day
and Marc Christian.

Still, I can dream my death,
and did, last night.
A taxi careening up Broadway
delivered me.
Alfred, Gordon, Laurent, David, and Adam
stood on a balcony
waving at something in the distance,
perhaps a tugboat
churning up the East River.
They didn't see me down here,
hauling my bags out of the trunk,
tipping the driver too much,
as I always do,
out of nervousness.

It's one of those cast-iron buildings
in the teens,
recently renovated,

sure of purpose
with dirty windows
and messengers rushing in and out.

Is it *my* building though?
I unfurl the Post-It
clutched in my fist.
It is.
I'm so tired
I can barely carry my luggage
(brought enough for a long stay!)
up to the revolving door.
The doorman
does not help,
but frowns at me.
In a whoosh of glass
and breath
I am in the door,
refracted and blurry,
spinning, spinning.
The strength of the guy behind me,
in an even greater hurry
to gain entrance,
slams the bottom of the door
into my heels.
Then the marbleized lobby,
the office-like hush.

Charles Barber

The Pamphlet I Threw Out

ARE YOU GAY? SCARED? DEPRESSED?
TIRED OF BARS? DOCTORS? MEMORIAL SERVICES?
DO YOU COUNT THE MINUTES YOU MAY HAVE LEFT TO LIVE?
ARE YOU LIVING IN A DREAM WORLD? A NIGHTMARE?

AESTHETIC SURREALISM IS FOR YOU

<u>What is Aesthetic Surrealism?</u> It sounds like a movement to turn gay men into melting clocks.

Aesthetic Surrealism is **not** a movement to turn gay men into melting clocks. Aesthetic Surrealism is a movement that recognizes that gay men have already become melting clocks. It is the only movement that considers the actual predicament we are in. When any hour we might awaken to a spot on our leg signaling the end, when any second our lungs may give out, what realistic sense of time can we possibly have? We constantly see time bending downward into the horizon. We watch as our friends' time on earth melts into nothingness. We wait to melt. We are melting clocks ticking out our own mortality. It is not merely time however. Our whole experience has become surrealistic in that it has taken on a nightmarish quality. When we make love shadows overwhelm us telling us our partner is murdering us. When we make love shadows overwhelm us telling us we are murdering our partner. Thus we masturbate more, alone, our hands covered with ants. We become Andalusian dogs sniffing our own asses in fear, slicing our own eyes to shut out the world around us. If this be our reality, let us embrace it. Let us not compound the fear by fearing it. Aesthetic Surrealism rejoices in our state as a scrap of bloodied cloth that a psychiatrist uses to cover one ear when he sees the patient who has nightmares about fornicating giraffes and weeping leopards. If we are windows covered in lips, let us be windows covered in lips.

You arrive at a meeting of Aesthetic Surrealism. As you step through the door you hear a blood-curdling scream. The room is filled with mannequins in torn underwear and men looking through microscopes. Suddenly you realize that the men are wearing torn underwear and the mannequins are looking through microscopes. A man you find attractive walks up to you. You go to hold him and he becomes a puddle of phosphorescent semen on the floor. You walk over to one of the microscopes. You look through it. You see yourself being hurled naked onto subway tracks. You look through another microscope. You see nothing, but the moment your eye hits the lens you smell an attic unused for thirty years. A bat flies above your head smashing through the window. The shards of broken glass grow legs and eyes. They become insects. Then they become tiny replicas of you.

If the preceding seems an accurate account of your life these days, you already are an aesthetic surrealist. There is no need to contact us in order to join. The dues are armpits covered in worms, or doorknobs with fingers. The meetings are every second in your mind.

Glenn Philip Kramer

I am the Loveless

i am the loveless
loving less
and what did you say on the phone last Friday
i putting the words together
like sequins on a bright velvet
round again
wishing i said less
you hurt
you with a whimpering voice
i in a web of self-pity
caught
you my spidery friend
weaving
and it snowing
fluttering flakes
sticking and gathering
white drifts
as high as white drifts
could be
i by the window
shivering
you a voice
too tropical for this
and i could kill
but pain shoots through
our lives
straight and direct as
a merciless arrow
round again
wishing i said more
your voice fading
as cold as snowdrifts

Tony J. Giordano

Ghazals in the Void

My friend laughs at me behind my back.
I turn around to duel the void.

Which drugs should I take? Which doctors should I seek?
My only recourse is to pool the void.

I wait for you to care in the next room
But even I can't fool the void.

Hot Mediterranean night, my body moist with longing—
I'll go bad if I don't cool the void.

The dervish spins his comic tale, a whirl,
Ever master of his tool: the void.

Since childhood, infinity confused me to sleeplessness.
Is thought an empty molecule? The void?

My doctor spoke impending death; lovers kissed in Central Park.
I thought and thought, how cruel the void!

I laugh and I laugh and I laugh again.
When did we first steal this jewel—the void?

The freedom the Ghazals give one to dance!
We feel almost as if we could rule the void.

Glenn Philip Kramer

Keith Haring, Deceased

Like a gunshot down an open street,
his finger on the trigger
tears a path in history's map.
Returning from the future,
consequence becomes reverse annihilation
forming him in lines and pictures,
values and portfolios.

Appreciation is collective consciousness,
the artist getting bigger.
Stronger than our memory's half life,
his finger on the brush and pen
has made a voice that can't be silenced—
timeless messages created
by his restless hand.

Invisible matter we produce
and then destroy, our sorrow in reflection
briefly gives existence
to the one who doesn't exist.
Sleepless nights bent on forgetting
feed the energy we spend.

And little can we say, or take away
from visionary consequence
projected from the artist's pen.

James Turcotte

Crayons

crayons
crayons
i need to color this day
splotches of red
running down my leg
i itch with color
i itch
words as pallid as chalk
thicken the air
color them hot
color them sincere
your brown eyes need bluing
my somber thoughts might
   burst
oh, god, i ache in rainbows
the hue is tremendous
your dark hair might grey
your lips need fullness
color the dog: wonder
color him running
color him yapping
sky
sky
skies of purple hurt between us
     above us
     beyond us
color it memory
color it now,
    then,
    sorrow,
    heartbreak,
color it laughter
your turn
my turn
crayons
crayons

Tony J. Giordano

74

Tomorrow Morning

What of the old chains
of love, laughter, fraternity
turned brittle, weak links
crumbling round my wrists
in this miserable daylight?
I've had it. Old bonds kept me
from tumbling off into some sky
blue adventure full of danger and
desire, geisha boys whimsically
singing the Hawaiian wedding
march as they interweave
baskets; Zulu tribesmen bearing
their long spears and stomping
feathered feet on the impacted
earth, thrusting broad pecs
at the sun, limbs akimbo; prewar
peasants in jolly jerkins making
bricks with their bare feet
straw and mud, all this national
geographic world spun out
on a platter before me. Now this
blinding sun reveals the casting
couch collapsing, the backlot
sold, the auctioneers come
and gone. Only the janitor,
his long handled broom sweeps
away this dream. Free at last,
free at last, not a shadow
anywhere in the streets.

Dan Conner

My True Desire

My insignificance seeks significance
From body to body,
From rubber to rubber
From cock to cock
Between cum-stained sheets
in a pair of white cotton briefs
Seeking the exhaustible relief
Groping the dark,
Groping in the light
Between my vomit and masturbation
And now during the incubation
Incessantly hoping,
Incessantly groping . . .

For God.

Raul E. Martinez-Avila

Tuesday in Holy Week, 1990, Dark Grey Day in Peekskill, NY

I

Surprised I am to be here.
Escaped from the city for a time.
Sitting on the grounds of St. Mary's Convent School
(Now converted condominiums with a view).
Gothic buildings guarding the Hudson's Tappan Zee.

Back along the cliff with far less view
Are the buildings of the remaining crew,
Standing stately, proud as Anglicans do.
Great stone barracks imposing
God's will on the citizenry about.

I wonder about Holy Week and Christ's Passion.
Why are there three nunneries here.
How can nuns have so much wealth
        and be so poor, so few.
Still Paschal Week pilgrims come to
Seek solitude in the peaks around Peekskill.

II

Under the shell of grand ostentatiousness
Likes the truth of the Passion.
        God is for us.
        We can be whole.
A presence need not be touched to be real.
Change can be wrought by a witness.
Care for strangers, the weak, the lonely,
        the poor takes many forms.
Patient observation of ancient rites
Moves a revolution of stalagmites.

III

My space is sketched by an unseen cartoonist.
Confined to the limits of those lines I am
Free to pump up or suck in the limits.
Space defined by a body.
My body, mine alone.

In it I am born and live.
No one can really pierce
to know my burden.
Many have penetrated
without breaking the lines,
loved and cared,
held my hands,
even conformed our shapes.
No one can really pierce
to know my pain.

"Jesus walked this lonesome valley.
He had to walk it by himself.
Nobody else would do it for him."
I have to walk it by myself.

Freedom Day.
The lines are erased.
The body no longer holds me.
Now I know life.

Glenn Besco

Fairy Book Lines

Death be nimble—
              life was quick;
Efficiency's a modern trope
To be expected
              with impatience
Not less
              when bearing death
Or a low-burning illness
              slow as memory
Though death's old-fashioned
              and enters the room
Like "Sonnambula,"
              bearing a burning candlestick.

Double, double
              toil and trouble;
Triple sadness,
              endless sorrow:
Like friends sitting too long
              by the hospital bed—
Like the T.V. watching you
              with paralyzing glare;
While the night-nurses
              in soft-soled shoes
Wheel in the confections
              to ensure your misery
Will last a long tomorrow.

The world's so full
              of a number of things
Now to be never savored
Never to fire
              a subordinate employee
Destroy a marriage
              position an M1A1 tank
On desert children.
Marveling at such achievements
              is a sure way

To gladly sacrifice
                a number of things
The world has always favored.

Poor old Charlie,
                he swallowed a fly;
The fly was drunk
                with M.A.I.
Buzzed here buzzed there
Till a well-seasoned fever
                stitched in hues
Of delirium-like gold,
                cooked in a broth
Of bacterium-stock,
                festering with forgotten dreams,
Took hold—took him—took life.

Twinkle, twinkle
                eyes in pain;
Retinitis makes
                its awful gain.
Eyesight's a form of breathing
                —like glass,
Full and rich with freedom.
Now a bag
                slides over the head
too bad!
                So long to the world
So long desired:
                darkness sucks you down its drain.

Fly away, fly away,
                over the sea,
Sun-loving sick boy,
                for summer is done.
First the pneumonia,
                canceling the lung,
Followed by a possible list
                of viral, bacterial, parasitical,

And let us not forget fungal,
The slow-covering growth,
          so like nature,
Slowly returning the body to earth,
          adrift in underground.

Charles Barber

What Happens

What happens
do we become dust
do we dance with friends gone
awaiting friends to come
do we walk the tunnel of light
are our sins shown to us
in horrific detail
do we play and contemplate
is there music
do we plan our next adventure
do we wail and lament
do we scream
is there love
do we become part
of a whole
is there laughter
do we become swirls of light
of energy
is there thought
is the stench of decayed flesh
ever present
in our nostrils
is there memory
do we become etheric bodies
suffused with joy
do we become travelers
enlightened messengers
sent to soothe the sufferers
of other dimensions
do we see our former life
through noble eyes
do we become dust

Glenn Philip Kramer

Death is Abstract

death is abstract
but the process of dying
is terrifying
and one can't shake off
those moments of
subterranean living
when a shadow prevails
and panic seizes
one by the heart and throat
and will not let go
this comes at night
at the turning off of lights
and the sounds of humming
alarm clocks, dripping taps,
footsteps above, nothing and
everything drums in one's ears
the pounding heart, the itching skin
gasping, gasping for breath
not now, now now one pleads
there are still ahead
days of living, whatever they may be
death is too abstract
one must have life, must live
must exist another day

Tony J. Giordano

III

OUT OF YOUR NAKEDNESS,
OUT OF MY NAKEDNESS

Out of Your Nakedness,
Out of My Nakedness

CONSISTING AS IT does of prose interspersed with poetry or poems connected by prose commentary, depending on one's approach, the piece of writing that follows eludes generic definition. In some ways it feels like a sequel to "The Lights Must Never Go Out"; but it would be truer to call "Lights" and the present essay complementary attempts to deal with the same material. "Lights" describes the poetry workshop I ran at Gay Men's Health Crisis beginning in early 1988. Quoting from the poems some of the clients wrote, it eschews the poems I myself was writing at the same time. True to the law of the return of the repressed, my own work is in abundant evidence in "Nakedness." But why the prose commentary in this second piece? Can't my poems speak for themselves?

Yes and no. My hope is that no poem here requires a single line of explanation in order to communicate. At the same time, these sixteen poems seem to me to be charged with a context that remains compelling even after their immediate occasions have faded. If this context was worth preserving, I reasoned, then such preservation required more than a succession of lyrical moments. A more detailed landscape was needed—a more detailed background, I almost wrote, but the poems are as much background as the prose.

This wish to preserve a context was new to me. In my previous books, trimming the circumstantial from my poems had been a crucial stage in the preparation of a manuscript. When enough work had accumulated, my practice was carefully to detach these poems from the various layers of living which had given rise to them. In order to fashion the fresh shape of the finished collection, I revised chronology and blurred narrative. True, this end product might still suggest consecutive, if veiled, incidents. But the aesthetic that governed the finished work was essentially one of exclusion.

The same reticence that is omnipresent in the arrangement of my previous manuscripts was probably what kept my own poems out of "The Lights Must Never Go Out." Rightly so; that essay, whose task is to evoke the workshop as it first developed, is no place for my own overflow. But after "Lights" was behind me, the number of my own poems on and around the subject of the workshop kept growing. It was impossible not to see these poems as a group which, if it didn't exactly tell a story, certainly traced a recognizable trajectory.

These, then, were poems that deserved—no, demanded—to be presented together. But a mere grouping was insufficient. The poems needed to be connected more fully than the obliqueness and impatience of the lyrical mode, as well as of my temperament, allowed for. Not—I repeat—that the individual poems gathered here are impossibly obscure. Rather, the very genre of lyric tended to mask or distort, by foreshortening them, the occasions without which these poems could not have come into being.

What were these occasions? They ranged from personal encounters—exchanges at the workshop, for example, or hospital visits—to the more inchoate stuff of fears and angers, dreams and desires. Of course such experiences are the raw material for most poetry. What was new was the urgent sense that unless these incidents and feelings were further explored by the person who knew most about them, myself, they would fade into oblivion. Before I ever saw the slogan of ACT-UP, an activist gay organization, "Silence is Death," I found myself equating utterance with life.

Before utterance comes knowledge. Yet natural as it seemed to think of my own experiences, emotions, and memories as a form of knowing, a flourishing tradition exists of severing poetry from knowledge. The matter of what and how the poet knows has been problematic ever since Socrates' sly protestation in the *Apology*:

> I used to pick up some of what I thought were their [the poets'] most perfect works and question them closely about the meaning of what they had written, in the hope of incidentally enlarging my own knowledge. Well, gentlemen, I hesitate to tell you the truth, but it must be told. It is hardly an exaggeration to say that any of the bystanders could have explained those poems better than their actual authors. So I soon made up my mind about the poets too: I decided that it was not wisdom that enabled them to write their poetry, but a kind of instinct or inspiration, such as you find in seers or prophets who deliver all their sublime messages without knowing in the least what they mean. It seemed clear to me that the poets were in much the same case; and I also observed that the very fact that they were poets made them think that they had a perfect understanding of all other subjects, of which they were totally ignorant. (21B–22E, translated by Hugh Tredennick)

"When it comes to poetry, every bourgeois is a Plato," said Joseph Brodsky in a recent lecture, referring to "the instinctive desire of every social order—be it a democracy, autocracy, theocracy, idiocracy, or mediocracy—

to compromise or belittle the authority of poetry, which, apart from ri-valling that of the state, hoists a question mark over the individual himself, over his achievements and mental security, over his very significance."

One broad form this "desire to compromise or belittle the authority of poetry" has recently taken is that of an attack on the very notion of meaning, let alone feeling or authorial intention, in literature. To explicate a text these days seems to many an old-fashioned exercise, redeemed from futility only by a dubious pedagogic value. And if this is true of literary texts in general, it is certainly true of poetry. A climate in which (the words are Ge-offrey Hartman's) "literature is precisely that use of language which can purge pathos" is the last place we should expect poems to be read with criti-cal attention—particularly if, as in the present case, the critic is the poet herself.

The poet-critic is an uncomfortable hybrid. Jovially but ruefully, Um-berto Eco has written that as a novelist who is also a literary critic and com-mentator on his own works, he feels like "both guinea-pig and scientist." Another image that evokes the author who turns an analytical eye on his own work comes to mind from Baudelaire's aptly titled "The Self-Tormentor," who is both *victime* and *bourreau*.

Executioner *and* condemned, white-coated technician *and* experimental animal . . . Although I don't feel as schizoid as such tropes suggest, the experience of writing prose about my own poetry has admittedly been a strange one. Perhaps I've been guilty of a kind of triple hubris: first, in presuming that my poems have merited this lengthy commentary; second, in presuming I was myself competent to write such a commentary; and third, in believing that close readings are appropriate ways to treat poems. Even if only one of these charges were to be brought against me, the process of writing "Out of Your Nakedness, Out of My Nakedness" has, as the title implies, been fraught with a sense of exposure and vulnerability. "I find it troublesome," Tocqueville wrote, "to discuss matters which interest me lit-tle, and painful to discuss those in which I am keenly interested." Precisely.

But this process has also been an education. The sixteen poems that form the scaffolding of this essay have far more to say, both separately and in cho-rus, than I was aware of when I wrote them. And Brodsky to the contrary, much of what they say does more to confirm than to question human achievements. For one thing, rereading my own work renewed my faith in the power of patient, attentive rereading to make a text leap to life. If the texts in question were my own, so much the better. I had something of the sense Robert Frost evoked beautifully when he described

> looking backward . . . to see how many poems I could find toward
> some one meaning it might seem absurd to have had in advance, but
> it would be all right to accept from fate after the fact. The interest,

the pastime was to learn if there had been any divinity shaping my ends and I had been building better than I knew. In other words could anything of larger design, even the roughest, any broken or dotted fragment of a figure be discovered among the apparently random lesser designs of the several poems?

I have written in "Lights" of how even a beloved passage in a poem can suddenly flicker disconcertingly in and out of focus, failing, as often as not, to provide us with what we had made the mistake of assuming was there. Yet at other times a single line on the page can light up the murkiest of moments. Lending itself as it tolerantly does to repeated approaches, allowing different moods, references, tones, and contexts, literature, as I discovered again, is an amazingly tactful and patient medium. Given the right attention, what was leaden and opaque can come alive with a captured lambency that would otherwise have been lost.

Reading brings us back to what has been written. And writing—this was another discovery or rediscovery—thumbs its nose at mortality. To be in the workshop was to be acutely aware of the ticking—now almost inaudible, now deafening—of the hidden clock in every life. One of our human choices is whether to speak or to be silent; the ominous ticking in the background simply highlighted that choice. Between the ghostly clock and the people in the room, all of us gradually interposed successive strata of language: the clients' poems, and my own poems, and lastly my commentary on these. Call it all a kind of insulation, in the form of memory and anecdote, against the chill and silence of death.

This image sounds stark. Yet the experience of the workshop has been a great joy for me. The joy reappeared in the writing of this essay: my initial hesitation at writing about my own poetry soon gave way to delicious repeated shocks of belated understanding. As I've put these poems together, the sense of rediscovery has been so strong that I have tried to ban from the following pages such phrases as "I now see that what I was doing was" or "what this line means" or "how these images connect." The leitmotif would have become too tedious, and besides, my aim has been to write calmly, without squeals of retroactive revelation. All the same, some sense of excitement may seep through what I referred to a moment ago as the layer of insulation provided by the prose commentary.

Perhaps this tissue of talk can be thought of as a kind of drapery that enhances, rather than muffling, the essential nakedness that the poems depict—that they even, I hope, enact. For the image of this nakedness I am indebted to Jane Cooper's powerful poem "Conversation by the Body's Light," the first lines of which have provided the present essay with its title. I am grateful to Cooper for beautifully showing how out of what seems to be nothing, something can be not only made but shared. I come back to "Conversation by the Body's Light" at the close of this essay.

A final word on how to approach this mix of poetry and prose. The sixteen poems here are presented roughly in the order in which they were written. Skip the prose commentary and you get a collection; skip the poems and something like a narrative is the result. But the alternation has its own rationale: out of the mixture something new may emerge. "Conversation by the Body's Light" puts it like this:

> Between the swimmer in the water
> And the watcher in the skies
> Something is altered

Taking Sides

Who wouldn't want to be elsewhere?
Afternoons I for one
would love to take a siesta.
And if the dream of horizontality
floats me off like a boat,
what tugs you two away I can imagine.
Nevertheless we're here,
students doodling at life's
dull and incessant lecture.

Our task today: to write against the clock.
Hush. The makework pastime
darkens to divination as we sit.
Can you make out the mortal
combat between twin wishes,
opposing poles of dumbness and of speech?
Each wants to win our trio
to his own way of thinking.
They hiss at us "This is for your own good!"

Dumbness desires the paper to stay white.
Language longs for dumbness
to open his mouth for once
and spill out the accumulated poison
into the tank of air,
into the bath of hours,
into the somber parody of a classroom
where we three bend our heads
and scribble away for life.

"Taking Sides" was written during and immediately after what I think of as the first phase of the workshop, in the spring of 1988. An early draft of the poem, indeed, was probably written at the workshop, where, as I've described elsewhere, we all did a good deal of writing around the table.

On Friday afternoons I was usually tired or at least sleepy, and all the preliminaries of the workshop—getting down to Chelsea, summoning the energy to do whatever presiding or directing I did—went a bit against the grain. I remember looking out the window on milky, hazy, damp afternoons in February, March, April, and letting my mind wander. If there was a faint flavor of school to the proceedings, a sense of "Okay, get out your notebooks," the opposite of this superegotistical mood also prevailed—the sense of an abstracted, dreamy undertow, a relaxed drifting toward oblivion.

In the context of AIDS, writing "against the clock" and "for life" immediately take on specific and somber connotations—something the poem seems aware of, although at the time it was written I hadn't yet heard about Michael Klein's anthology (then in progress) *Poets for Life*. But more distinctive than the sense, however poignant, of mortality's invisible presence on the scene is the way "Taking Sides" posits the contest between life and death as a quarrel between speech and dumbness, "opposing poles" which are sketchily personified as rival therapies, angry parents, or just contrasting human impulses stubbornly planted at opposite ends of the table.

In this poem the urge to speak out—in anger or in fear or simply to bear witness—is overdetermined, as indeed it is in poetry in general, and certainly in poetry written under the shadow of the AIDS epidemic. "Silence is Death" is a phrase I hadn't yet heard at the time "Taking Sides" was written. But in my mild-mannered, sometimes schoolmistressy way, I seemed to have been anticipating ACT-UP's provocative slogan.

Silence—whether it's construed as the suppression of other people's speech or hopelessness about one's own words making any difference—is cynical, easy, and false to human nature. "We are human beings," writes Montaigne in his essay "On Liars," "and we have relations with one another only by speech." This notion is elaborated in a twentieth-century context by Primo Levi in *The Drowned and the Saved*:

> According to a theory fashionable during those years [the 1970s], which seems to me frivolous and irritating, "incommunicability" supposedly was an inevitable ingredient, a life sentence inherent to the human condition, particularly the life style of industrial society: we are monads, incapable of reciprocal messages, or capable only of truncated messages, false at their departure, misunderstood on arrival. Discourse is fictitious, pure noise, a painted veil that conceals existential silence; we are alone, even (or especially) if we live in pairs. It seems to me that this lament originates in and points to mental laziness; certainly it encourages it, in a dangerous vicious circle. Except for cases of pathological incapacity, one can and must communicate, and thereby contribute in a useful and easy way to the peace of others and oneself, because silence, the absence of signals, is itself a signal, but an ambiguous one, and ambiguity generates anxiety and suspicion. To say that it is impossible to communicate is false; one always can. To refuse to communicate is a failing; we are biologically and socially predisposed to communication, and in particular to its highly evolved and noble form, which is language. All members of the human species speak, no nonhuman species knows how to speak.

"Silence, the absence of signals, is itself a signal, but an ambiguous one," Levi comments. But if ACT-UP is right, there is little ambiguity in the silence that so often muffles the subject of AIDS. Simon Watney opens his eloquent book *Policing Desire: Pornography, AIDS, and the Media*, with a passage from Iris Murdoch's *The Fire and the Sun* which is congruent with Montaigne's and Levi's thoughts on the conflict between silence and speech:

> The careful responsible skilful use of words is our highest instrument of thought and one of our highest modes of being: an idea which might seem obvious but is not now by any means universally accepted.

Watney uses Murdoch's words in the ironic context of the shamed, evasive silence that muffled the mourning at the funeral of a friend. This man's parents, Watney writes,

> had been condemned to silence, to euphemism, to the shame of guilt by association, in this the most devastating moment of their lives as parents. I . . . decided there and then that I would write a book on the subject of AIDS.

In this embattled context, the message of silence is clear and deadly.

"Taking Sides" construes language as either speech or writing; the line "Dumbness desires the paper to stay white" conflates writing and speech as twin weapons against muteness. The intentionally overbearing tone of "This is for your own good!" is an admission that speech and silence both, like rival doctors, claim that their methods of treatment are salutary (the talking cure versus stoical silence). But in the context of AIDS, all silence offers is oblivion. As Montaigne and Levi so eloquently attest, speech, by insisting on our social nature as human beings, allows the possibility of communicating with a larger group even if the individual is doomed.

The question of the individual and the group is evident in the use of pronouns in "Taking Sides." Before the first stanza is over, "I" and "you" seem to have become "we." How did I dare to say in effect "I am one of you?" In the same way that, a year later, writers demonstrating outside PEN headquarters a few blocks away would chant "We ARE Rushdie!"

I return to the image of the white page. The Greek poet George Seferis's beautiful late sequence *Three Secret Poems*, written in the sixties, evokes the mood of isolated existential gloom that makes Primo Levi so impatient. But if I read Seferis rightly, he is not saying that we are condemned to lonely muteness. Rather, what we need is the courage to fill the white sheet; if we can do that, then the "harsh mirror" will end by giving us back something. Seferis is eloquent on the riskiness of utterance, the daring needed to write down anything at all. But is there any alternative?

The white sheet of paper, harsh mirror,
gives back only what you were.

The white sheet talks with your voice,
your very own,
not the voice you'd like to have;
your music is life,
the life you wasted.
If you want to, you can regain it:
concentrate on this blank object
that throws you back
to where you started.

You travelled, saw many moons, many suns,
touched dead and living,
felt the pain young men know,
the moaning of woman,
a boy's bitterness—

what you've felt will fall away to nothing
unless you commit yourself to this void.
Maybe you'll find there what you thought was lost:
youth's burgeoning, the justified shipwreck of age.

Your life is what you gave,
this void is what you gave:
the white sheet of paper.

> (George Seferis, from "Summer Solstice," from
> *Three Secret Poems,* tr. Edmund Keeley and
> Philip Sherrard.)

The Lenten Tunnel

You kneel and retch and pray,
gargle for help in the dark,
weak as a child. Unlike a child
in lowering your sobs
not to awaken the beloved sleeper,
you give the finger to what
blocks air, chokes you like a locomotive.

You last the darkness out.
Not quite dawn yet, but night
exhausted, colors seep
back into bed and table,
into M's sleeping face,
into your arms, your hands,
and finally the mirror,

the specter through whose terror
you daily find the strength
to put yourself together,
your own familiar gaze
piercing the patchy pallor.
Morning. The child whose dreams
I'm privileged to hear

told me today a comet,
luminous, streaming, last night
filled the sky of his sleep.
You say the end of your tunnel
brims with radiance.
Whatever flows, I answer,
must have found a channel.

Borrowing favorite phrases from another person's work makes it easier to
see oneself in that person's poem. In this sense, the "harsh mirror" of Seferis's
white page mercifully turns out to reflect more than one thing at a time.
Sometime before Easter 1988, Kevin's phrase "the lenten tunnel," with its
suggestion of a redemptive light on the far side of earthly suffering, was put
to use in a draft of a poem Wayne was writing, though I can't find it in any
of the worksheets I've kept. Later that spring Wayne died. When, in the sum-
mer, I wrote an elegy for him, it felt right to use a phrase that had, so to speak,
been appropriated already and so was part of the common stock.

"The Lenten Tunnel" imagines the end of a night and beginning of the next morning late in the (or a) sick man's life. The detail of being violently ill in the night and of trying not to wake his sleeping lover is one Wayne told me; the sense of choking in the dark, and the fact of returning daylight making lesions visible again, I imagined. Meeting one's own eyes in the mirror and finding a kind of strength there is an important idea in a sequence Wayne had not yet finished when he died, but the image also has a source in my past bouts with insomnia, when, during the long, disembodied night hours, seeing my familiar face in the mirror was oddly reassuring.

Wayne wrote somewhere, probably in the draft I've lost, that there was light at the end of his tunnel. Or was that Kevin's line—or both of theirs? Unfortunately, the light at the end of the tunnel in my own poem feels unearned and sentimental to me. My son's dream of a comet fitted the theme of luminosity nicely, but it doesn't prevent "The Lenten Tunnel" from ending on much too easy a note of transcendence—an ersatz uplift which, like cognac in espresso, "Elegy Variations," the next poem, may do something to correct.

I'm all the more aware of the shortcomings in "The Lenten Tunnel" because this poem appeared in *Poets for Life*, a book where one can find many poems that take far more uncompromising looks at AIDS and death.

Elegy Variations

I   Tears

Tears in themselves are not a test of love.
Call them the weeping, as a sore can weep,
of some fresh loss. They also signify
the precious rising sap of memory.
They water the green region of a smile.
They help to navigate the caves of ice
and float us through dim arches to a place
where pairs of mourners in the smoky air
lean toward each other as if their desire
were one enfolding for eternity.
No: the embrace
of shadow flesh in an embodiment
of truth we come to late as we approach
that shore, our sluggish senses
thickening even as they seem to stretch.
Mourners, but mourners who must stay in motion,
we tip out tears, libation in the dust,
a few dark drops for the road,
and turn to trace the paths of separation.

II   Parting

I knew no better answer than "don't cry"
to your "I love you" when we said goodbye.

Oh stubbornness and mercy of the earth!
Instinctively affections reattach
their hopeful suckers as the spring returns.
Spring pierces this pale room, so many blades
of light between the blinds.
I could have said "I've never trusted sun
in March; this year it's extra treacherous."
I hadn't come to talk about the weather.
To be there was to have entered a procession
halted as frieze. You in the center; M
on one side held your hand; I on the other
stroked your long legs, touched your big right foot,
still calloused from your work, still flexed for more

dancing; apart, one shoulder to the wall,
your father, standing closest to the door.

Our places taken, not much need to speak.
Belatedly the flaws of winter break.

III   The Voice

The letters smear the sky,
are scrawled over the gates.
No ambiguity:
they spell out IRON AGE.

But black winds bleed to white.
Sleep spreads the floor like fleece.
Who wades across this threshold
enters forgetfulness.

Echo, hour, echo:
gongs tremble, speak,
finally awaking memories
even in those who lack

reckoning. Take me—
I grope for where you are.
Yet your loss whisks the dustsheet
off my heart's desire.

Now I recall the quiet
deep waters of your will;
I see the garish sunlight
glazing the gritty sill.

Gallant at your going
you held yourself upright,
tilted toward what you said
goodbye to: light.

Tell me, was it despair
that spoke in a frozen voice,
or did the voice of winter
disguise itself as love?

"Elegy Variations," written a little later than "The Lenten Tunnel" in the
summer of '88, seems to be dealing with unfinished elegiac business. Like
the earlier poem, this three-part sequence rummages in the ragbag of

phrases that was one legacy of the workshop. The first line of "Tears," Part
I of "Elegy Variations," I owe once again to Kevin. "Tears in themselves are
not a test of love"—this lachrymose, faintly Tennysonian line he came up
with by itself, suggesting that it might be a good first line for a poem.

Fooling around with the line, I spun out a set of metaphorical variations
on what tears might mean, moving none too logically from more to less hu-
manly eloquent kinds of fluid: a weeping sore, rising sap, a navigable
stream, a libation. Between the stream and the libation is inserted a cameo
scene of a lovers' farewell that recalls Orpheus and Eurydice or some other
classic pair.

Despite its stately diction, "Tears" implicitly argues against the sen-
timental notion that tears possess a redemptive magic which dissolves differ-
ences and erases boundaries. The mourners here "must stay in motion" and
end by moving apart "to trace the paths of separation." Tears cannot
miraculously reunite them. On the other hand, mourning has brought
them together (think of the last scene of *Romeo and Juliet*). Unlike the iso-
lated, silenced mourners at the funeral that goaded Watney into writing his
book, these mourners are consciously "we."

Another classical reference surfaces: "the embrace/of shadow flesh" re-
minds me of Odysseus trying to embrace his mother's shade in the under-
world, and failing. The very section of *The Odyssey* that vividly depicts an
afterlife also underlines the physical finality of death. Mourning and tears
cannot bring back the dead.

"Tears in themselves are not a test of love." What did Kevin mean, any-
way, by this ambiguous line? One sense I get is that tears alone are no proof
love exists. "Not a test": not a criterion? "In themselves": perhaps tears are
a necessary but not a sufficient indication of love's presence. In "Parting,"
the central section of "Elegy Variations," the opening couplet immediately
and uncomfortably juxtaposes tears and love:

> I knew no better than to say "Don't cry"
> to your "I love you" when we said goodbye.

Because "Parting" draws on my sole hospital visit to Wayne (which was
also the first in a series of hospital visits to several people), it is probably a
truer tribute than the rather factitious farewell in "The Lenten Tunnel."
Whereas "The Lenten Tunnel" is, as it were, spoken smoothly (if not
smugly) after the fact, "Parting" preserves, at least for a line or two, some
of the abrupt illogicality of a spoken exchange.

Farewells are never easy. And my memory of this particular farewell, to
a pallid man with a tube in his nose, who began to cry as I moved toward
the door—or was he already crying?—is painful in more ways than one. I
felt, and feel, so helpless, so separate. I had cowardly impulses to make

small talk, but I knew "I wasn't there to talk about the weather." Why then was I there, when there was so little I could apparently do? Sympathy, empathy, even company: all these notions refer to some kind of parity, when what I felt was more a sense of strangeness.

Long after this farewell visit, I found some abstract consolation in Bakhtin's luminous insights on the nature and limits of human communication.

> Understanding cannot be understood as emotional empathy, or as the placing of oneself in another's place (the loss of one's own place) . . . Understanding cannot be understood as translation from someone else's language into one's own language.

Still, how *are* we to understanding understanding? In "Parting" — uselessly but not wrongly — I take myself to task, after the fact, for my inability to truly answer Wayne's words to me. "Don't cry" comes perilously close to an adjuration to silence. Why on earth should a dying man *not* cry? Wayne's tears suffused his already emotional words with more feeling without making them unintelligible. I clearly heard a phrase it isn't often given to adults to hear, and all I did was scuttle out of the room, embarrassed, unequal to the situation, muttering an inadequate, platitudinous phrase for farewell. By replaying the scene that led up to this farewell, "Parting," as poems do, mitigates the harshness of what happened by allowing me, if not quite to relive the scene, then at least to rewrite it.

I'm quick to think of other mitigating factors as well. I didn't know this was the last time I'd see Wayne. And like most people, I hadn't had much practice at deathbeds. My father died suddenly in Colorado when I was seventeen and grounded in St. Louis by a plane strike; even had the planes been flying, there would have been no time for a goodbye. The memorial service at Columbia a few months later was imbued with the presiding spirit of the university. My father's professional life had center stage, and there seemed no intimate place to retreat to — not even any assurance that the renowned teacher and scholar who was being publicly eulogized was the same person as a stunned adolescent's father.

Why do we write elegies? Is it the other person's death we are mourning, or is it our grief for ourselves? In his "Consolation of Helvia," Seneca writes to his mother:

> Since, my dearest mother, there is nothing in my situation to drive you to endless weeping, it must follow that your impulse to tears derives from your own situation.

Granted, Seneca is referring to his own exile, not his death. But the psychological acuity remains. My friend Mark Rudman recently wrote me on the occasion of his stepfather's death:

It's not known how much of the mourning is for ourselves potentially or for others but we mustn't cleverly underestimate the latter. Others come to dwell in us. They become part of our cells, within our cell.

Certainly "it's not known" to the mourners themselves how the grief is generated or apportioned. In making hospital visits, in running the workshop at all, I may well have been trying to fill the gap still left by my father's death (and I'll have occasion later on to discuss further his quirky concept of a "much-needed gap").

Insofar as the focus of the elegy was the man in the bed, not myself, it didn't—doesn't—matter what I said or failed to say. Why should I have an adequate answer to words which, like Wayne's tears, probably resembled gestures made almost at random to the years of his own past life as, like harried visitors, they sped out the door? What could or should I have said?

Knowing I would never know for certain, I seem, in writing "Parting," to have concentrated on what I did know. Harold Bloom tells us in *Ruin the Sacred Truths* that "Remembering is, in poetry, always the major mode of cognition." For months I remembered that room in Lenox Hill well enough to draw a diagram of it, which is more or less what "Parting" does. The careful description of who stood where, no less than the belated apostrophe, is an attempt to recover lost time by looking backward intently, missing nothing.

The image of the "procession / halted as frieze" troubles me a bit. It's uncomfortably clear that the central figure on the altar, the precious destined sacrifice held and stroked on either side, is the man in the bed. Does "Elegy Variations" make a Keatsian claim for art as a the sole fixative in a world of flux, illness, and death? "Tears," after all, depicts "pairs of mourners in the smoky air /[who] lean toward each other as if their desire/were one enfolding for eternity," rather like the permanently poised lovers early in "Ode on a Grecian Urn." "Parting" offers a darker version of this scene, a funereal triptych: man in bed, lover on one side, friend on the other—and cruelly marginal father off to one side, muffling his face like a relief sculpture on an Attic grave stele.

Since the sick man is not a figure on a Greek urn but a person, Wayne McCarthy, who died in April 1988, what good does all this encapsulating do? Who is the audience of the poem? Who are its beneficiaries, if any exist? In any approach to an answer, the human urgency of bearing witness converges with art's power to tell the truth. Even if the truth does no good, trying to tell it is a way of combatting the sinister mandate of dumbness that the paper remain white.

Howard Norman, the novelist and translator of Cree Indian tales, has described interviewing an elderly Cree woman during the brief Arctic summer. It was crucial to talk to her before the ice closed in, ending transportation and communication for another year. Summer in that latitude, I remember Norman saying, lasted eight days. The woman was old and frail; by the following summer she would probably be dead, and there would be one less native Cree speaker to pass on the traditional stories.

If AIDS is a language, we are tragically far from running out of speakers—indeed, the opposite is true. Nevertheless, the human urgency of the need for bearing witness holds. Not the paucity of speakers but the multitude of sufferers threatens to overwhelm everyone with silence; and it is this threat that I am concerned to combat. To repeat Primo Levi's words, "One can and must communicate."

Each of the three sections of "Elegy Variations" can be seen as an intensifying revision or recapitulation (what Northrop Frye would call an antitype) of what precedes it. Thus "Tears" unpacks its own first line; "Parting" focuses on a particular example of the kind of painful occasion more abstractly evoked in "Tears." The final section, "The Voice," further investigates the problem of speech and meaning which comes up at the start of "Parting" but is still, in that section, secondary to the spectacle of the frieze.

"The Voice," which begins with a written message and ends with a "frozen voice," asks whose this mysterious voice is. No answer is given, but we can provide a few—the epoch's, the poet's, the sufferer's. "Taking Sides" has prepared us for the fact that "The Voice" starts with an image of writing: "The letters smear the sky, / are scrawled over the gates." In our time the witness's, commentator's, and poet's voices all are likely to work through writing; must be deciphered like writing; come after the event, like writing. "No ambiguity," proclaims the poem; yet the images that follow are hardly crystalline. They lead dreamily to a realm of stark oppositions, envisioned as a weirdly interchangeable black and white. The poem seems to enter a place of oblivion; then an echo—akin to a voice—brings back the original pain of loss.

As I read this hermetic poem now, I am neither paraphrasing nor translating my original ideas or images back into clear and simple prose. There never was any such clarity; all I can do is feel my way. "I grope for where you are"—this line expresses some of the frustration of the process, as well as recalling the bewilderment in the face of death and absence that I first expressed in an elegy to my father: "So far away / and never farther than my arms and legs / and never coming back." For if meaning is being sought, so is the actual vanished body of the beloved person who has unaccountably disappeared to death. Maybe the meaning *is* the body, or vice versa.

Paradoxically, but true to the laws of mourning, absence and loss reveal what has been masked till now: "Your loss whisks the dustsheet / off my heart's desire." The unveiling of desire allows, finally, for a replaying of the scene of loss that lies behind "The Voice." Although this scene has already been evoked once in "Parting," now this last section stubbornly conjures up again the bright spring day, the hospital room, the figure in the bed.

For the living to question the dead is as venerable a poetic prerogative as for the dead to address, exhort, or warn the living. The question asked at the end of "The Voice" is oblique, although as communication it's an improvement on "Don't cry." To use the relevant verb again, this question *gropes* toward a dichotomy that may reflect the earlier image of black and white: was it X or Y? But it's characteristic of the dreamlike quality of "The Voice" that oppositions, instead of being formally set up, tend to be huddled together, stirred, melted, so that black can "bleed" to white. Thus, at the end, despair, winter, and freezing can find themselves in the vicinity of love—the same love Kevin began by grouping with tears, or the valedictory love bravely voiced by the man in the bed.

The Revenant

A strange particularity
shapes this man asleep
beside me, whose least curve
I thought I knew by heart,
knew in my bones, knew inside
out (Greeks say *ap'exo*,
from outside in). But no:
the pulled-up knees and slender
ankles of a dead dancer
animate the dreaming
tenant of his body.
From near, from far
ghost and guest converge
to one form so familiar
it leaves love open
wide to forgery—
to the illusion that it doesn't matter
whose long-backed grace
is folded between these sheets,
what person, incognito,
either masked in blankness
or curled to fit the contour
of a former self
shares my bed. It's no
illusion life and death
are intertwined as any loving sleepers.
To be so beloved
must he not be familiar?
Fondly familiarity
breeds blindness: recognition
comes to be lodged
in loving touch alone.
I shut my eyes,
pass my fingertips
over the body
of the nameless breather.

Written around the same time as "Elegy Variations," "The Revenant" is yet another meditation on death. Here, though, rather than an occasion (such as a hospital visit) which demands a certain protocol, death is felt as a condition. The condition is primarily one of absence, but also, unsettlingly, it is a state of mind or even body. "The Revenant" considers a posthumous presence. But instead of addressing its ghostly subject with the familiarity lyric poets have always airily appropriated, "The Revenant" is careful to maintain a kind of impersonality. It derives its immediacy as utterance from demonstrative pronouns ("this man asleep beside me") and the present tense, but "the nameless breather" is never directly spoken to, precisely because, without identity, his fugitive spirit can be deceptively molded into a familiar form.

Of course the revenant has identity in a way. The "slender/ankles of a dead dancer" may recall the long legs and "big right foot/still calloused from your work, still flexed for more/dancing" of the central figure in "Parting." Here again there is a hint of funerary sculpture, the supine grace of a recumbent posture. But in another way, identity is erased. Although the sense that it doesn't matter who one's neighbor in bed is is called an illusion, a "forgery," nevertheless recognition in this poem is achieved, paradoxically, only through blindness. In other words, the relation of depth to surface is scrambled. "The Revenant" tries for a deeper eradication than that in "Taking Sides," where "I" and "you two" melt into "we," or even in "Parting," where the various people in the room are somehow united into a mute tragic chorus ("Our places taken, not much need to speak"). Under attack in "The Revenant," albeit a dreamy attack, is the boundary not only between self and other but between inner and outer.

"From near, from far/ghost and guest converge" punningly echoes Gerard Manley Hopkins's "Spring and Fall":

> Nor mouth had, no, nor mind, expressed
> What heart heard of, ghost guessed:
> It is the blight man was born for,
> It is Margaret you mourn for.

What the two poems share can be fumblingly explained as a nonrational form of cognition, an inarticulate thought whose burden is a dim sense of profound neighborliness, of shared mortality.

Almost asleep, curled to the contour of my husband's body, I sensed his long back and slender legs as being somehow also those of a man I had certainly never lain down next to but had last seen when he was lying down. Wayne? Of course; but the experience also echoed an earlier episode which involved blurred identities.

Twenty years ago, involved with two different men, I wasn't always sure whom I was embracing. One night, I and one of these men found ourselves sharing our train compartment with a third person, an Englishman returning sadly home to London after a failed attempt at reconciliation with his

Greek wife. We all lay down to sleep, parallel, close together but not impossibly crowded. I must have been in the middle, for deep in the night I became aware that the Englishman had wrapped his arms and legs around me, and that I in my sleep had been hugging him just as hard. Who knows who each of us thought or dreamed the other was? Such nocturnal confusions are probably universal. Still, the burden of "The Revenant" is not so much universality as—equally uncannily—human uniqueness, the "strange particularity" that "shapes this man asleep."

"To be so beloved/must he not be familiar?" is a question which resonates beyond the sexual, psychological, or literary (think of Ishmael and Queequeg, or Whitman's loving hugging bedfellow) into the realm of politics and morality. Who is my neighbor? The question is both simpleminded and very difficult. Christ prefers, in Luke's Gospel, to tell the parable of the Good Samaritan to spelling out an answer. As soon as one dives even a little way beneath the surface of consciousness, such questions abound. Who is my beloved? my student? my child? Who is the man in bed with me? Whose is this ghost?

Such blurring and converging identities, constantly "scissoring and mending," in James Merrill's memorable image of a boat and its reflection on the water, are, I suspect, a part of human experience many people prefer not to talk about—too murky, embarrassing, confusing. Like the lovers at the end of *A Midsummer Night's Dream*, do we not wake up at last to one another's true identities and leave behind such dreamlike misapprehensions?

Not necessarily. When it is a question not just of sleep but of death, these nocturnal confusions are forms of visitation, of survival, no more to be dismissed than another, more durable medium of survival—language.

Less Than Kind

SYPHILIS SURGE AND CRACK USE RAISE AIDS FEARS
Queasily breakers burst:
headline half gibberish, half storm at sea.
Escaping public weather, I retreat
to the remotest corner of the lawn
(mock orange blossoms fragrant even here):
and what do I tote to the hammock as my tutor?
Facts I thirst for, history as atrocity,
syphilis surge and crack or worse than these.
Fear, hunger, war, plague, deathcamp, cruelty:
formerly herded under some umbrella
epithet like "inconceivable,"
the host of demons does not seem so strange
to me now swinging, reading
of them with more than simple recognition,
with—yes—a kind of longing.
Anatomize this leaning toward the *crack*
and surge, this almost putting out a hand.
Is discerning evil's
face in this verdant corner
a vague desire to avert
one more repetition of a cycle
(knowledge as prophylaxis) or the thrill
catharsis shoots through calmest summer skies?

Driven to articulate
abstraction into faces we might make,
we read our kind. The kinship's dim but deep.
More than curiosity, not quite memory,
but as a language newly learned uncovers
glassy blocks that shape a pyramid,
its shining structure inch by inch revealed,
so piece by piece the bad
news takes shape and is not
surprising; was always there;
was necessary to know.
and crack use stir Or just the fascination
that moves a child to study hurricanes,
earthquakes, tornadoes, twisters,
takes hold of us perusing our own pillage

scaled to human uses *raise aids fears*
Metaphors we thought long dead take on
a phosphorescent half-life of their own:
raging illness expressed as rough sea,
verbs spume to nouns in general anarchy,
emerging sleekly sea-changed: aids as death.
The nightmare mirror smashed to tiny shards
patiently pieced together through the long
eventless hours of a private summer:
finally a human
figure emerges, to a cry, if not
of triumph, of accomplishment
or recognition's deep perennial pleasure.

"Less Than Kind," written at about the same time as "Elegy Variations" and "The Revenant," nevertheless seems not to belong to the same cluster. In its rather generalized, abstracting approach to its theme — the fascination exerted by evil and suffering — "Less Than Kind" has more the air of a prologue to or comment on other poems than of a poem itself. In fact, it's simply speaking in another register. Often in my work, if I have no particular incident to chew over, I turn to contemplate the ever-present and ever-enigmatic medium itself: language. Here, the *New York Times* headline — "Syphilis Surge and Crack Use Raise AIDS Fears" — which serves as the poem's first line was also its occasion. "Less Than Kind" begins by noticing the vigorous metaphor generated (unintentionally?) by the combination of the words (both verbs scrunched into nominatives) "surge" and "crack" and then goes on to take a look at my, and "our," human appetite for knowledge of disaster.

The source of such knowledge isn't merely a sensational headline, for these were the hot weeks in June and July '88 when I was spellbound by Primo Levi's books about the Holocaust. As if for comic relief, my son during those same weeks kept asking for books about tornadoes, hurricanes, volcanoes — natural disasters, but still disasters. Earlier in the spring, a children's book purporting to be the account of a journey to a black hole had been one of the very few stories to frighten him at bedtime. I couldn't help being struck now by the relish with which an elderly library book about tornadoes described the roar of a twister, the dirty yellow light before it struck, and the way sofas or silos, roofs or cows might be briefly visible inside the funnel before being sucked up to oblivion.

Strong stuff, all of this, especially in contrast to the green lawn, shady hammock, and uncluttered hours which seemed by their very leisure to invite me to take such scenes in. Why, though, when people supposedly hanker after escapist reading in the summer, were such subjects so compelling?

"Less Than Kind," if it doesn't fully answer this question, manages at least to ask it. The title may hint at an answer. Its three words come from the first line spoken by Hamlet. In a sneering response to Claudius' just having publicly addressed him as both "cousin" and "son," Hamlet mutters, "A little more than kin, and less than kind." *Kind*: our contemporary sense of "nice, thoughtful, generous" overlays the Elizabethan meaning of "natural" or "related." Close but far, like but unlike, intimate but treacherous — these are some of the oppositions Hamlet's nine words manage to suggest. "Less Than Kind," too, ponders the question of kinship, wondering what the public world of hideous human behavior has to do with a shady summer lawn. Another possible answer also uses the word "kind": Donne's resounding "Every man's death diminishes me, because I am involved in mankind."

The poem considers epistemology — how it is that when we "read our kind" we perceive "kinship," "dim but deep." Our relation to the world of the Lager as described by Levi, or to the crack users described in the *Times* article, or indeed — coming closer to home — to people with AIDS, is or ought to be one of kinship. We are not gawking at an irrelevant past or at alien others. One might say rather platonically that even the most sheltered person has a dim familiarity with the idea of a tornado, an epidemic, a concentration camp. Of course any such familiarity, however fugitive, means — and here I think I am parting company with Platonic Ideas — that we were taught or read or told about these things. In other words, someone bore witness. Hamlet adjures Horatio at the end to "tell my story"; Primo Levi more than once compares himself to the Ancient Mariner, compelled periodically to tell the tale of his wanderings to listeners who, however unwillingly, "cannot choose but hear." Somehow they know the story concerns them.

I was never as well instructed in math as the slave boy in the *Meno* from whom Socrates so suavely extracts a geometrical proof. But my experience in learning French and Latin is the basis for the passage in "Less Than Kind" beginning "But as a language newly learned uncovers/glassy blocks that shape a pyramid. . . . " Something like that sense of the gradual unveiling of a preexistent and inevitable structure accompanied each step of my acquisition of knowledge where the laws of language were concerned. Is this phenomenon of a piece with the fact that I can't now remember never having known about AIDS? Of course there was a time when no one knew; but why, when the syndrome has become a daily word in our lives' glossary, is it so hard for me to pin down the first time I heard of this new illness and began inadequately to imagine what it might mean? Because it takes death to drive things home? Significantly, the recent film *Longtime Companion* is divided into incremental portions, in each of which the characters learn more about the disease even as it steadily thins their ranks. The viewer, knowing more from the start, feels both more knowledgeable and more hopeless than the people on the screen.

The blaring headline that starts "Less Than Kind" reduces by the end to something utterly unfrightening—a mere human figure. "Recognition's deep perennial pleasure," an idea familiar since Aristotle at least, is crucial when we come to grant human parity to another person. It takes a sense of recognition to be able to acknowledge the validity of another's experience, and the acknowledgment, in turn, enhances the sense of recognition. Also required, of course, is a willingness to communicate; someone who chooses not to tell his or her story can get no recognition.

In the *Poetics*, where he also speaks of recognition, Aristotle distinguishes poetry from history. History, he says, tells us only what has happened; poetry speaks of and to the much more capacious category of what might, what could happen. The kind of knowledge with which "Less Than Kind" concerns itself is located somewhere between history and poetry. Historical catastrophes were real, past, public, attested events, but they can always recur; we have no cures for war, earthquakes, genocide, new epidemics. In fact there is a seamless continuum between what happened and what could happen. It's no accident that, seeking an authoritative voice suitably steeped in ironic knowledge, Simon Watney chooses to end his book on AIDS with a quote from Thucydides on the plague—that same Thucydides who tells us early on that his book will be useful in case, as he expects, similar events transpire in the future.

September

Without referring to its opposite,
September's crystal spins upon itself.
Only internal symmetries

garble flaws and leer along the light,
glassily yielding nothing up
but riveted reflections, mended cracks.

Recurrent elegy
pins us to the pleasure of the moment
from whose danger something solemn swells.

A single shark fin scores a honey sea,
silver through gold, the carnivore's profound
amber of saturated sentiment.

Standing on the shore, we spy a distant
ridge of disquiet swelling like a scar
over the halcyon surface. For a storm

is brewing. Queasy secrets strain to break
their bonds. In this centripetal and roiling
richness any one of us could drown.

Platform

Dim world, we stand and wait,
crane along the edge
to see the coming train.
Having first tucked away
those who have fallen or even
stumbled, we proceed
to stride the clean streets of our simple lives.
Shall I tell you a story,
something about debility, about
contradiction? We who share
a city with the wounded
avert our gaze from the ripest contradictions.

Hard to start a story with no ending.
Long days, long dialectics, and long waits.
Long silences. Beyond the beckoning
warning lights of the oncoming train
public demeanor yields up nothing more
than a numb wariness.
Still, little spurts of lightning
spit along the tracks,
linking absent gazes, looping arcs
across the net of past and present, stretching
progressions (friendship; understanding; illness)
out like taffy strands in lurid light.

Since the workshop was in abeyance for academic 1988–89, the remaining eleven poems date from the months between the fall of '89 and the fall of '90. As a matter of chronology, "September" comes first in this group and "Platform" months later, but it makes sense to place and discuss these two poems together, in part because they share as theme and image the sense of an edge.

"September" takes its stance on a shore, "Platform" on a subway platform, but both poems are tinged with the equivocal security of a safe-haven feeling, the snugness of a spectator watching storm-tossed seas from a discreet distance. The locus classicus of this image is the proem to Book II in Lucretius' *De Rerum Natura: "suave mari magno* . . . " Of course the safe spectator is looking out not just upon the sea but at life, with its unfathomable passions, complexities, and dangers.

A direct source for "September" was a recent performance of my husband, George Edwards's, trio for horn, violin, and piano. In wildly unmusical terms, what I heard was something like silver and gold harmonies combining to create a dense envelope of sound—a rich surface beneath which something piercingly sharp was barely concealed. The aura was oxymoronic: luxurious peril, hazardous comfort. That nothing is quite safe, and that nothing is what it seems to be: themes from "Less Than Kind" or "The Revenant" resurface here, although now draped in almost hieratically elaborate diction.

"Less Than Kind" considers atrocities calmly, from the safe harbor of the hammock. But "September" is piqued, almost to prurience, by the secret dangers of whatever is out there, that "ridge of disquiet swelling like a scar." The halcyon surface is in fact "centripetal . . . any one of us could drown." The wish to dive deep into the unknown, whatever the attendant risks, suffuses "September" like a slow blush, and also like a prophecy of the coming year, when my hours at GMHC sometimes seemed to leave the familiar coasts of the land of poetry workshops and venture out to uncharted seas.

"Platform" recapitulates the idea of an edge, but this time the spectator stands not on some sketchily imaged shore but inside a subway station in a city full of pain and suffering. "Platform" began as a response to a sight I ended by crossing out of the poem itself. The first lines came into my head late one afternoon at the end of May, when, on the last leg of my trip home from Newark, I found myself waiting for the uptown IRT in the sleek Cortlandt Street station beneath the World Trade Center. A man sat propped against the token booth; his outstretched legs, swollen and pocky, made his illness, rather than homelessness or poverty, seem to be on display—if the distinction made any difference.

This man was relatively unobtrusive. That he wasn't upright, let alone mobile, made it easy to walk away, or to pretend not have seen him at all. Besides, since all the people waiting impatiently on the platform daily saw dozens of people begging in stations and on the street, we knew what he signified without even having to look at him.

Something in the station's very spiffiness seemed heartless and antiseptic. Was it the low ceiling, the backless benches, the shiny tile walls, the streamlined silence of the train itself when it finally pulled in? All this order—it was suddenly obvious—could only be achieved by the tucking away of whatever offensive elements disturbed the public symmetry. Moreover, everyone felt free to ignore the single beggar in the station because we were ignoring each other too. As if in response to this conspiratorial muteness, an inner voice demanded sardonically, "Shall I tell you a story,/something about debility, about/contradiction?"

Like sideways glances, the "little spurts of lightning . . . along the tracks" break up the ruthless forward motion of the oncoming train. It's even as if they relieve the deathly stillness. These flashes recall, probably too strongly, the "points of light" (recently revived by President Bush's speechwriter Peggy Noonan in the guise of "a thousand points of light") from Auden's great poem "September 1, 1939":

> Defenceless under the night
> Our world in stupor lies;
> Yet, dotted everywhere,
> Ironic points of light
> Flash out wherever the Just
> Exchange their messages. . . .

But anterior to the image of those flashes, as I wrote the poem, was the tantalizing and unfulfilled promise of narrative: shall I tell you a story? The poem reneges on its own promise with the excuse "Hard to tell a story with no ending"; the flashes are at most incidents, anecdotes, not real stories. They serve as generic markers: this is a poem, not a narrative. Yet this brief poem, as if dissatisfied with the platform it's perched on, suggests that there are stories to be told about debility and contradiction—that the impatient onward motion of the train leaves a lot behind.

At the end of "Platform," the little flashes become more ambitious as means of communication, seeming to grow and reticulate until they form a net "linking absent gazes, looping arcs." If "Platform" had an epigraph, it might be Forster's "Only Connect"—two words which apply just as well to this entire constellation of poems.

October

October Thursdays. Circle of pale men
living their lives ahead of the unknown
allotted season, day, or afternoon,

hour, minute. (Achilles to Lykaon:
"Morning or midday, friend, my time will come.")
A waxy light pervades this basement room,

windowless; even so,
they always see as far as corridors
allow until a certain unmarked turn.

Lips twisted with Achilles' irony,
they straddle living bodies, tangled, warm;
they brush aside the doomed

ransom-bearer's feebly flourished gold.
Wait; it is themselves they wave away.
The bodies they bestride here are their own.

By the end of October '89 the workshop was meeting every week in a basement seminar room in the slick new GMHC quarters on Twentieth Street. If a windowless basement sounds like a privation, this is misleading; it was a luxury for everyone to have a room with chairs, a table, a door that closed.

In "Taking Sides," my earlier poem specifically about the workshop, the pronouns move from "I" and "you two" to "we." "October" restricts itself to the third person plural, as if the people in the room were being described by an observer with a one-way mirror. The poem begins in a matter-of-fact way, but ceases to be straightforward as soon as it broaches a topic of overwhelming importance to everyone in the room: time.

"October Thursdays" establishes a schedule, meticulously placing the event in a predictable grid. Months, days, times of day seem unproblematic, though the "pale men" strike an ominous note. By the second line, the question is no longer where precisely one is located in time but the more challenging one of how to move through it. The men are said to be "living their lives ahead of the unknown," a curious concept: how does one do that? They may be sitting in a "circle" around the table, but their separate lives can only move forward in isolation.

At the first couple of meetings in the windowless room, the "circle" consisted of myself and one new client, Charles. It must have been at our second meeting that, in response to a question I asked about his poem, this young man said something that struck me as more important, altogether larger than his tidy lyric about snow—so important that I scribbled his words down on the xeroxed manuscript of his poem. Typically, I can't lay my hand on that piece of paper now. But I know the sentence I wrote down was about death, time, and knowledge—the certainty as to what, the uncertainty as to when, and the resulting problem of why, rather than how, to go on living. This terrible question is one that, like the letters in the first stanza of "The Voice," "smears the sky/is scrawled over the gates" of everyone whose life is touched by AIDS. If a deity can be imagined in the interrogative mode, the question became a sort of household god, presiding in the windowless room. When? In the meanwhile, how? Above all, why?

In Book XXI of *The Iliad*, a Trojan named Lykaon begs Achilles to spare his life. Lykaon offers Achilles a lavish ransom; he can afford to, being one of Priam's bastard sons. Adding to the poignancy of Lykaon's situation, at least in his own eyes, is the fact that he has already been captured once by Achilles but has been ransomed. Now he has had the bad luck to fall into Achilles' hands again—an Achilles whom the death of Patroklos has made utterly merciless. This new Achilles answers Lykaon's plea:

"Idiot," said he, "talk not to me of ransom. Until Patroklos fell I preferred to give the Trojans quarter, and sold beyond the sea many of those whom I had taken alive; but now not a man shall live of those whom heaven delivers into my hands with the sons of Priam. Therefore, my friend, you too shall die. Why should you whine in this way? Patroklos fell, and he was a better man than you are. I too—see you not how I am great and goodly? I am son to a noble father, and have a goddess for my mother, but the hands of doom and death overshadow me all as surely. The day will come, either at dawn or dark, or at the noontide, when one shall take my life also in battle, either with his spear, or with an arrow sped from the bow. (tr. Samuel Butler)

From several standpoints, this speech is one of the great moments in *The Iliad*. It signifies Achilles' relentless awareness of his own mortality—an awareness that enables him to address the man he is about to kill as *philos*, friend. After all, aren't they, as two men condemned to death, in the same boat?

There is a bluff realism, too, in Achilles' tactless, perfectly matter-of-fact enumeration of the many ways he, the son of a goddess, is superior to Lykaon. Not that superiority in size, strength, or beauty makes any difference. For the detail that most struck me when I first encountered this passage, and which is probably still my favorite, is Achilles' offhand but, again, realistic speculation as to exactly how and, above all, exactly *when* he will be killed. The spear or arrow will strike him either in the morning, afternoon, or evening. It's not that there are no questions about Achilles' eventual death; there are assuredly more possibilities than exist in poor Lykaon's extreme case. The point is that the essential knowledge of the outcome is not in doubt.

A passage in Nabokov's *Pnin* refers to a Pushkin lyric which I have not been able to find in translation, but whose preoccupation makes it a close relative to Achilles' speech:

> In a set of eight tetrametric quatrains Pushkin described the morbid habit he always had, whatever he was doing—dwelling on thoughts of death and closely inspecting every passing day as he strove to find in its cryptogram a certain "future anniversary": the day and month that would appear, somewhere, sometime upon his tombstone.

At times, in the windowless seminar room, the idea of death usurped the foreground. At other times the people in the room, with their memories and experiences, took over the foreground and the knowledge of mortality retreated. When "October" speaks of "waxy light" in a "basement room, windowless," the imagery takes on a tomblike cast, as if to acknowledge the ubiquity of the idea of death. The "branching corridors" with their "certain unmarked turn" originate in metaphor rather than in the physical layout of the building, yet these corridors, too, are easily imagined in terms of mortuary architecture—subterranean tunnels, say, in a pyramid.

The men who joined or rejoined the workshop as the fall went on—Charles, Glenn, Kevin, Tony, Raoul, James, Dan—seemed to be a self-selected group of people willing, in the words of the poem, to come into contact with a grisly pile not of corpses but of "living bodies, tangled, warm." The needs of the living prevailed, as they had to. Though some beautiful elegies did get written, the workshop was no cottage industry for elegy. "October" nowhere refers to tears or mourning. The poem depicts no vale of tears but—taking its cue from the tone of the workshop—a tougher place, not without courage and also, as is frequently true in Homer, not without bitterness.

Courageously, then, and sometimes contemptuously, the living reject a ransom, "wave away . . . the proffered gold." Are they then, like Achilles, determined to kill? Here the thought of "October" doubles and tangles. Like Achilles, they refuse a ransom; like Achilles, they are doomed themselves. "It is themselves they wave away./The bodies they bestride here are their own."

The image of bestriding a body has both erotic and warlike elements, but more crucial here, perhaps, is the sense of personal doubleness ("beside myself," we say) that sometimes transforms human perception. Don't we, in entering the mind of another person, as in reaching beyond ourselves to love, manage to hoist ourselves up onto our own restrictive bodies? "The human creature," Stevie Smith writes, "is alone in his carapace. Poetry is a strong way out."

In a figure as distant yet familiar as Achilles, I recognized the uncanny sense of having outlived oneself—another kind of doubleness, another climbing atop one's own body. At one moment, you struggle with the more or less healthy or suffering body you inhabit; at the next moment, a sudden distancing permits you to look back down on your own remarkably removed life. A passage near the conclusion of "The Harrowing Plunge," Larry Josephs's account of his struggle with AIDS, illustrates precisely this distanced doubleness:

> I see a life that must be enjoyed today, now, while I am healthy enough to enjoy things. I see friends and relatives who must be cherished now, today, because they may soon become shadows in my life. Or is it I who will become the shadow? (*New York Times Magazine*, 11/11/90)

Something like this unsettling access of perspective, which affected everyone in the workshop at different times, is what Baudelaire describes in *"Le Goût du Néant"* when he imagines himself sitting on top of the world, looking down with cold indifference:

> Je contemple d'en haut le globe en sa rondure,
> Et je n'y cherche plus l'abri d'une cahute.

> The round world turns below me—distant sight;
> I want no mountain hut to keep me warm. (my translation)

Baudelaire's image of frigid distance takes on a more benevolent, though still an extremely detached, tone in Giacomo Leopardi's description, in the *Pensieri*, of what happens to the person in exile:

> Being divided from mankind and almost from life itself has this advantage: even though a man is tired of the world, even though experience has enlightened him and put him out of love with human affairs, yet little by little he grows used to gazing at them from a distance, whence they appear far more beautiful and valuable than from close at hand. He forgets their vanity and wretchedness and begins to form and almost create the world after his own fashion.

Of course the sense of removal, of disembodiedness, of suspension need not lead to recreating the world. It can as easily spell terror, depression, rage. Still, the dismantling of what had seemed like solid structures gave the workshop a strange atmosphere of wreckage (there was one poem about

119

a tornado), of the ruins of a used-up world. Would anything emerge from it? "I wish I had a new body," said Raoul suddenly one day. In a memorable phrase, he calls his body, in a poem, "my borrowed cage."

Of course the sense of outliving oneself is a kind of mourning—for others, for oneself. Achilles feels its full force after Patroklos has been killed: he misses his beloved friend and also knows his own death is that much closer. Seen from one angle, Achilles' foreknowledge of his own death gives him a tragic splendor. But from the vantage point of daily life, that world where it is morning or afternoon or evening, it steals the savor from the present. Sandwiched between Patroklos' past death and his own future death, Achilles sees no reason to eat or sleep. All that feels right is killing.

At some point in the fall, Charles told me that at his support group, which met in a similar windowless room in the basement, if not in the identical one, people often spoke of the torment of living in a situation nobody had foreseen. A person with AIDS could live longer now, perhaps, but forever with the knowledge of his sentence. Surely, I wanted to say, they were grateful for extended lives, new treatments, ever-present hope? Maybe it was at the thought of Achilles and Lykaon that this insipid consolation died on my lips.

Transitional Objects

Clock or mirror, teddy bear or fountain:
how comfortably we settle upon emblems!
Yet with what almost desperate discretion
we pry up surfaces without discarding
the merely seen. Steamy morning mirror
or threadbare animal or questing gaze—
I understand at last all these are not
recklessly to be peeled
off still raw, tossed scornfully aside
in search of buried treasure.
My old impatience with idolatry
loosens its bodice, takes a breath, makes do
with what is given. If appearances
are less than everything, still they are something
to be first lingered over and then looked through.
No, both at the same time.

It was probably in October that I gave a workshop assignment based on
the Rilke selections in Kenneth Koch's *Sleeping on the Wing*, the anthology
we used a good deal. The brief essay on Rilke that accompanies Koch's selec-
tions from the poetry suggests that Rilke's poetry gives voice to inanimate
objects—a notion that may be reductive as far as Rilke's oeuvre goes, but
was stimulating for the assignment that immediately suggested itself: write
a poem to, or about, or in the voice of an inanimate object. People leaped
at the suggestion.

"Transitional Objects" slightly sourly wonders why. It comments on the
alacrity with which people chose totems, emblems, mascots to identify
with—Glenn's teddy bear, Kevin's clock, Charles's mirror . . . I myself
started a poem addressed to the fountain near Saint John the Divine where
I liked to wait before picking up my son at the end of the day. Perhaps it
was because this poem never really worked that I felt an inchoate irritation
with the whole notion of speaking to or through a thing. Yet the idea was
a fruitful one. The associations that came up were—predictably—as reveal-
ing as those in the game of Freudian Botticelli, where Jane Austen is a tea-
cup to Ernest Hemingway's beer stein, a settee to his bar stool. Glenn's
teddy bear, for example, was an amusing alter ego for this big ursine man,
but the choice meant more than that: people hospitalized with AIDS very
often clutch teddy bears.

As the title "Transitional Objects" indicates, I associated all these alter
egos with D. W. Winnicott's notion of beloved toys or blankets that help

to wean the small child from the mother's presence. Was everyone weaning himself? A few weeks later, around Christmas, I asked for poems about family and was greeted with a chorus of groans (the groans were even louder on Valentine's Day, when I had the lack of imagination to ask for poems about love). But the poems that chose and addressed or spoke as surrogates seemed to be not only fun to write but also productive gestures of self-definition, as well as being metaphoric workouts.

"Transitional Objects" blows off a little steam by acknowledging first the fact of my discomfort with mere "emblems" and then the fact that "if appearances/are less than everything, they still are something/to be first lingered over and then looked through."

Looked *through*: does the visible but opaque carapace of things grow transparent, then, with time? In poem after poem, my 1983 book *Slow Transparency* affirms exactly that. I now think the answer is both yes and no. We look at things until we can see through them, but in this world the things themselves are still there. Nabokov in *The Gift* beautifully captures this sensation, which he calls

> multilevel thinking: you look at a person and you see him as clearly as if he were fashioned of glass and you were the glass blower, while at the same time not in the least impinging upon that clarity you notice some trifle on the side . . .

Czeslaw Milosz has the same double vision in mind, I think, when he writes "There is so very much death, and that is why affection for pigtails, bright-colored skirts in the wind, for paper boats no more durable than we are."

Teddy bears and clocks and mirrors seem very durable in contrast to Milosz's rapid array of ephemera, and maybe I was unreasonably irked by this very solidity, as if it were sentimental and false. A little more thought about Rilke might have disabused me of this notion. Transformation as he presents it is no parlor game, yet there is something of the conjuror's trick in his magical way of turning something inside out and triumphing at the feat, or recommending metamorphosis as if it were the easiest thing in the world:

> Move through transformation, out and in.
> What is the deepest loss that you have suffered?
> If drinking is bitter, change yourself to wine.
>
> *(Sonnets to Orpheus II.xxix,* tr. S. Mitchell)

Laments

Jenny Holzer installation,
Dia Foundation, December 1989

Twilight seeps into this empty room,
garage, or attic, and the moon shines in.
Perched on a pew (this is the protocol),
one watches words stream past, a waterfall
beaded with light; then in the inner room
paces around the same words stuck in stone.
Too many messages come pouring in—
interrupted feasts, a trip by train—
though many slyly sheathe themselves in dreams
affectionate and kind and tinged with shame.
Sharing—that eucharistic fantasy
through which our isolated spirits try
to touch some surface shivering like skin . . .
As in a dream the signs slide glittering past.
Their crucial message, both the first and last,
is "What we are is also what we say:
marble neon incessant elegy."

You and I once more prowl the inner room.
It's smaller; shedlike. History's dark barn
swept clean—are words the sweepings, or are we?
Does this whole faintly humming warehouse say
we've painted ourselves into a corner of
utterance? A long lament for love
finds its form first as inscription,
archive to epitaph to taph to tomb,
a recapitulation of our need
to set down phrases mourning our fresh dead.
Half sham-archaic Back to Basics, half
heroic unknown soldier's cenotaph;
logos or logo scribbled on the flat
affect of our postmodern habitat.
The letters whisk down; pause; start up once more.
Radical erasures flicker here.
Abstracted, next to you I sit, gaze, wait
for the electric shimmer to abate.
You say my eyes will get accustomed to

the dark; but since the symbols
keep pulsing to crescendo, guttering out,
sparking afresh the cool
stutter of silence, tape-loop troped as jewel,
nothing is constant, and they never do.

In the cluster that starts with "September," six of the seven remaining poems—"Laments," "The Solarium," "Fin de Siècle," "Half in Love," "The Green Wall," and "The Sleeping Beauty"—constitute a formal and thematic subgroup. Formally, all these poems are in the second person; thematically, all revolve around this same person. Charles—the first client to join the workshop that fall—and I became friends. The poems that follow can be read as a tracing of our friendship; perhaps they can equally be thought of as half of a dialogue the other half of which was often never written down.

If this group had consisted exclusively of intimate utterances, they might not belong in this collection. But besides marking the development of a friendship, these poems can also be seen as continuing to map the world of AIDS. From a trip to an art gallery to the ways people talk about the millennium, my exchanges with Charles seemed to give me new insights into what I am not the first to call the way we live now.

At a more prosaic level, Charles was the person who accompanied me to Jenny Holzer's installation "Laments," and it was Charles I visited in the "solarium" of a hospital. Yet it is precisely because he is a very shadowy figure in these poems that I feel free to include them. Sometimes, in them, he seems like a conduit, a synecdoche channeling a range of thoughts and feelings into utterance, an articulate emblem with a pleasant human face.

Whatever intimacy these poems convey may signal a corresponding loss in objectivity—if we believe poems ever are objective. Undeniably, the wary, apparently deadpan spectator/narrator of "October" or "The Revenant" has now given way, for better or worse, to an altogether more vulnerable and engaged voice, which broadcasts its involvement by consistently addressing a "you."

Nevertheless, behind the "I/you" exchange and very much coloring it, are the same familiar questions that come up in many of the other poems—the same wranglings with mortality, knowledge, and love. The AIDS crisis did not create these questions, but for me as for many other people it has presided over them, reshaped them, given them a fresh context and a deadly urgency.

"Laments" ponders a visit Charles and I made at his suggestion to a Jenny Holzer installation of that name. It was the last week of 1989, a clear cold evening; as we left the workshop, the moon was shining. The Chelsea streets looked very festive, with little holiday lights and warmly glowing interior scenes visible through tall windows.

This was the pretty cityscape we walked through, but the installation, when we got there, was singularly lacking both in seasonal good cheer and in the atmosphere of gallery glamor I had been vaguely expecting. Jenny Holzer's work has been repeatedly described elsewhere, and "Laments" attempts to evoke it again, maybe because when we arrived at the large, gloomy, almost empty space in the Dia Foundation, the place (it's hard to find a word for it; my poem tries with "room,/garage, or attic") wasn't at all what I had pictured.

There was a churchlike feel to the proceedings, owing not to the season but to what Gaston Bachelard has taught us to call the poetics of space. A bench against one wall looked like a pew. We sat down silently, Charles a bit hunched up, as if for warmth, in his black leather coat. Vertical columns of moving letters climbed, flashed, vanished, began again. What the letters actually spelled out was surprisingly, annoyingly pretentious and banal; as far as verbal inventiveness went, Holzer's offerings were like a gloomy reprise of Kahlil Gibran. Her aphorisms mourned the passing of the body, pleasure, freedom—but flatly, not acerbically. I neglected to write any of them down at the time, and none has stayed in my memory.

Like a codicil, the smaller of the installation's two rooms both clarified and revised the large neon version in the outer room. In here, eight or ten marble or alabaster sarcophagi, engraved with the same words that glittered next door, were lined up fairly close together, as in a smallish cemetery. The little room was very murky, but the marble surfaces were spotlit from above. As in a cemetery, one felt sanctioned to walk among and between the tombs, pausing to consider an inscription or compare styles of lettering or colors of stone. The sarcophagi varied a good deal in size, but none bore names or dates; probably cenotaph (empty tomb) is a more accurate term under the circumstances than sarcophagus (flesh-eater).

Obviously, my response to the installation was and remained an ambivalent compound of mystification, resistance, and a sneaking, cloudy sense of revelation. Holzer's message (I should have noted the central installation was purportedly "about" AIDS) seemed shallow and self-evident, yet her medium (a nod to Marshall McLuhan, whose spirit was in the chilly air of the place) was thought-provoking. My own thoughts, such as they were, concerned not AIDS but the nature of written language, the special properties of the inscribed alphabet, the special ways one reads letters carved in stone.

It was probably on this occasion that the poem I was to call "Fin de Siècle" began to take shape, for a feeling of ends and beginnings permeated this place. A mood that was becoming familiar both from the workshop and from many conversations with Charles prevailed here too: a sense of belatedness, of having outlasted one's own generation and world, met and grappled in this dark barny area with a sense of the archaic origins of writing in the West. Lest one miss the point, Holzer had juxtaposed these archaic inscriptions with the glitzy pyrotechnics of Times Square neon. Looking from one room to the other, I found myself thinking of Heraclitus's gnomic sayings, which may be fragmentary by accident or design, and of the many fragmentary inscriptions I had seen around the Heraion in Samos or at Ephesus.

If the neon strip letters with their fluorescent glow and pervasive buzz were postmodern in their showily cool effect, then the static carved versions of the same words in the smaller room presented themselves both as archetype and afterthought. Which version was true? Both sets of lettering pushed at the limits of my ideas of writing, both earliest and latest; in both, text superseded speech. The dim rooms were very quiet. The thing to do was look.

The mysteriousness of the installation was both pretentious and appealing. I was reminded of rural Greek churches, where one enters a dim space and lights a candle for private reasons—sins repented, beloved dead. In a way, what Holzer's presentation meant was in the eye of the beholder. But whatever that beholder did, "Laments" seemed to resist the old enemy, that "dumbness [that] desires the paper to stay white."

The visit to "Laments" continued to resonate. A few months after seeing the installation, I came across the following passage in Norman O. Brown's curious book *Closing Time*:

First the age of the gods, then the age of heroes, then the age of men. The origin is sacred; the decline is secularization, process is profanation: I sometimes think I see that civilizations originate in the disclosure of some mystery, some secret; and expand with the progressive publication of their secret; and end in exhaustion when there is no longer any secret, when the mystery has been divulged, that is to say profaned. The whole story is illustrated in the difference between ideogram and alphabet. The alphabet is indeed a democratic triumph; and the enigmatic ideogram . . . is a piece of mystery, a piece of poetry, not yet profaned.

And Holzer's show might have pleased Ezra Pound, whose importance in the above passage "ideogram" should alert us to. Her aim, perhaps, is to make it new *and* old by investing the democratic alphabet with hieratic strangeness. One's eyes do not grow accustomed to the darkness because the darkness keeps shifting, and so does one's vantage point. "Are words the sweepings, or are we?"

The Solarium

I

Christmas 1989. Ceaucescu
Executed. Billy Martin dead.
No sooner has the world been told
Of any public figure's sudden end
Than private meanings multiply
Around a life lopped off.
Call it myth. And is it also myth
That sitting next to you
Here in this hospital—ghostly straddler both
Of the East River and of the year's end—
Not only do my eyes
Dazzle at so much sky
But sunset's orange afterimage
Reads me back my life?

My life . . . No pronoun enters reverie
With half the clarity of the golden
Line where your neck and shoulder
Meet at the T-shirt's tear.
Nevertheless what the solarium
Gives me back is 1969:
Clean Monday in Peiraeus. Lenten sun.
Promises, lambent, squint to dissolution,
Erasing boundaries and spilling over
The many-windowed river to the sea.
In their wake invisible graffiti
Crosshatch sunset, myth, and memory.

II

One day a week at most one sees a peacock.
But day by day and week by week life deepens;
Hence the chaotic massed bewilderment
Of feathers heaped like refuse in a corner,
Too many feathers—all stiff stalks, round eyes.
It takes a retroactive effort
Even to try to imagine
The splendor of a single widespread tail,
Then from that tail, unique, a rigid plume
Plucked and brandished, gleaming and alone.

127

Why doesn't life as lived from day to day
Feel more like an accumulation?
The answer is it does, but we don't notice
Until events abruptly give us back
The single feather, overlooked, forgotten.
Thus the solarium this afternoon
Fills my eyes not only with late light
But how past waters, longing, rose toward sunset.
Whenever I can glut my gaze with sky
And drain my head, I leap the grey dream-wall
Where the poor pride of peacocks
Is crushed to something serviceable, dull.
Familiarity's faint glint
Glances off half a lifetime of utensils
Before they slip away
Into the world of the invisible.
An airborne traveller looks down
At the landscape she is leaving.
This tiny icon's the last thing she sees:
A tilting faded face
Screwed up for one last kiss.

III

Now in this late rooftop's copper sheen,
Radiant young man who stands between
Me and invisibility,
How can I reach you floating in the air?
Or who am I to net you
In wisps of stale desire?
Words stained russet with the afternoon
Will have to bear the burden,
Speaking in patient silence to the one
Who lowers his eyes to read.
Or tarnished feathers, leaves torn off unread
Lie in a deepening pile
Over the earth's cold bed.

A day or two after our visit to the Holzer installation, Charles went home
to Cleveland for a holiday visit. When he returned to New York he went
straight into the hospital, where, early in the New Year, I visited him.
"Solarium" tries to capture the peculiarly dreamy flavor of this winter af-
ternoon.

There was, to start with, the sense not of hurrying away but of linger-
ing—almost malingering. At "Laments" I had wanted to sit abstractedly in
the dark room for longer than life's responsibilities permitted, and here at
Co-op Care, on the top floors of the NYU Medical Center, it was the same
thing. Charles's presence was the common denominator—or was it his ab-
sence? In both places I could sit almost as if alone with my thoughts and
gaze out at an evocative but also an unobtrusive scene, all the while sub-
merged in "multilevel thinking." Here the scene from the solarium was the
winter sunset over the East River; from Charles's room, on the other side
of the building, was a closeup view of the Piranesi-like old Bellevue Hospi-
tal. January light etched everything with clarity at the same time that it
magnified distances.

On Christmas day, earlier that week, Billy Martin's death in a car crash
had elicited from my friend Mark Rudman a detailed poetic account of a
game in the late fifties in which he had seen Martin play. Not that the poem
was "about" Billy Martin; rather it was the latest in a series of what Kenneth
Burke might call representative anecdotes about Mark's own childhood.
What struck me was the uncanny way a public figure's abrupt death had
enabled Mark to pull such a big fish from the depths of the forgotten.

Ceaucescu, a very different kind of public figure, had of course died the
same day. I think I was musing about public deaths and private myths—
indulging in a fantasy scenario of Ceaucescu, Madame Ceaucescu, and Mar-
tin in some *No Exit*-like place—when, on this visit, I sank into an armchair
and stared out at the cold copper-colored sky. Up there on the top floor of the
hospital, one seemed to be floating as far above the world of life as above the
world of death—a sort of *Magic Mountain* illusion. Another illusion, since
Co-op care is for ambulatory patients, was that Charles and the other people
I saw were all perfectly well, perhaps enjoying a luxurious winter cruise.

"The Solarium" reverses the windowlessness of the scene of "October"—
this place was all windows. What I saw out those windows was not only the
river, helicopters, and sky, but kaleidoscopic fragments of my past. Trans-
lating Baudelaire's "Les Bijoux" recently, I've come across his notably glassy
image for the soul's tranquil but alert state:

> . . . le repos où mon âme était mise,
> . . . le rocher de cristal
> Où, calme et solitaire, elle s'était assise.

> . . . my soul's repose,
> The crystal rock where, calm and solitary,
> it was seated. (my translation)

I picture the soul perched like a lookout on this sparkling rock; the safe ha-
ven is also a vantage point.

"Laments" refers in passing ("interrupted feasts, a trip by train") to a self-explanatory dream I had recently had in which Charles got off a train before he and I had reached our destination. "The Solarium" too, after initially setting the scene on the top floor, pauses at a dream image. Several mornings a week all fall I had walked my son to school, and sometimes, once inside the Cathedral Close, we would see one of the precinct's peacocks. Such occasions felt special, for the peacocks, always somewhere around, were not always visible. My dream presented me with a crushed mass of peacock tail-feathers tossed like refuse from a high wall into a dark, dirty corner of the lawn—as dark and dirty, in fact, as the pigeon's nest I saw every day from my studio window, on the opposite sill.

The fugitive idea I'm following here is that of singling out one from many in order not so much to appreciate as to see at all. Yet those many morning walks, those repeated glimpses of peacocks—was this tarnished image all they amounted to? The "tree of many one" in Wordsworth's Immortality *Ode* tries the same trick, salvaging from the repetitions and accumulations of middle age something emblematic yet memorably unique. At the same time, Wordsworth's tree and "single field that I have looked upon" bring back the very waste and loss he is lamenting, for "Both of them speak of something that is gone."

Nor is the peacock dream that surfaces in the reverie at the solarium the poem's first recovery of a memory. In Part I, winter light reflecting on the river brings back seaside lenten strolls in Peiraeus twenty years earlier. To catch such unexpected glimpses of one's own past is a free gift—or not so free, since accompanying the past memory and the present moment is a sense of something fugitive and fleeting. "Familiarity's faint glint/Glances off half a lifetime of utensils/Before they slip away/Into the world of the invisible."

Invisibility may mean just what it says, unseeability; or it may mean oblivion (of great swatches of one's own past, like the vast bulk of one's dreams); or, finally, death. The "radiant young man" who occasions this flood of memories, or seems at least to preside over it, has almost been forgotten; Part III gestures toward him, but trying to reach him is like attempting to catch an angel in an earthly net. The images end by taking a nosedive from the sunset sky to "tarnished feathers . . . in a deepening pile/Over the earth's cold bed."

The feathers are piled like leaves ("leaves torn off unread"): leaves of grass? Or autumn leaves with their promise of renewal after months of cold? The poem reaches out in several possible directions without reaching any real conclusion, since what's placed at the close has the tentative feel of something parenthetical. As "Platform" puts it, "Hard to start a story with no ending." "The Solarium" looks easily back in time; to look ahead is another matter.

Fin de Siècle

Impossible to read a paragraph
These days and not to stumble over some
Reference to imminent millennium:

Sensation less of drowning than of draining.
Not one of us who wash around the sluice
But feels the suction. In a recent letter

F. writes of having "finally turned the corner
Into the postmodern," and I picture
A brisk back being turned upon a life

Left stranded on that corner ever after.
Future was once horizon; now it's angle
(Cavafy's angle to the universe,

Said Forster). People also speak of cusps:
Peaks, monstrous teeth or moons or mountain ranges.
Near you I sense no draining,

No corner turned, climacteric, finale,
No grandiose gesturings toward 2000.
It's January; and a few green leaves

Shadow your light eyes like the hope of summer,
A picnic at the swimming hole, a walk
Among wildflowers at the quarry's edge.

The opening lines of "Fin de Siècle," which like "The Solarium" dates from January 1990, scarcely exaggerate. Everything I saw in print those days, from a recipe to a book review, managed to drag in "some / Reference to imminent millennium." "Millennium" used — to my mind — to be vaguely synonymous with "apocalypse," but as we approach the year 2000, the entire bundle of associations accompanying any idea of millennium is being worn threadbare by sheer familiarity.

"Fin de Siècle" tries to take stock of what I imagine when the phrase or the subject comes up. Are we on a cliff, at the end of the world (*suave mari magno*), and will the new year, decade, and presently, century and millennium wash over us? No; the feeling is more like swirling around before going down a drain. There's a subliminal reference here, probably, to John Ashbery's image in "Self-Portrait in a Convex Mirror" of a sand descending in an hourglass:

The sands are hissing
As they approach the beginning of the big slide
Into what happened. This past
Is now here.

Of the last-quoted sentence David Kalstone has noted in *Five Temperaments* that "Four of these five monosyllables—"this past is now here"—point to the present with all the immediacy of which English is capable, and *past* disarms them all."

Another moribund metaphor of the kind poetry can oddly galvanize back into a semblance of life—and one closer to the phrase "turn of the century"—came to hand in a letter my husband had recently received. "Turning the corner into the postmodern": I imagined the very busy writer of the letter striding off into an ill-defined future (assuming "postmodern" connotes some kind of future) and leaving behind not only the inherited cultural conglomerate but also his wife and three small children like so much abandoned luggage on the sidewalk.

In E. M. Forster's book on Alexandria there's a famous cameo of Cavafy, "a Greek gentleman in a straw hat, standing at a slight angle to the universe." But to stand at an angle is not the same as turning one's back. The whole idea of *turning* "darkens to divination" (to borrow a line from "Taking Sides") as I consider it. It signifies change, maybe separation. One turns the corner, thereby turning away from those who have not yet turned the corner. In "October," the men in the labyrinthine basement are said to "see as far as corridors allow/always until a certain unmarked turn."

The change always associated with the idea of millennium is closer to us now in time, and of course brings anxiety with it. What will happen? Will we turn a sudden corner into a cul-de-sac? The poem glances at a few common images of transition, all strenuous evocations of ardent feats or at any rate of steepness.

Then "Fin de Siècle" itself takes a turn, in its last few lines, to a much simpler and more humanly scaled way of imagining and feeling, which turns out to be thinking of and addressing a single other person ("apostrophe" equals "turning-to"). Suddenly there is no occasion for threatening scenarios, there is only human time, in which life is measured not only by millennia but also by January and summertime, vulnerability and hope. "The hope of summer": looking forward to summer, to its leisurely warmth, as all the people in the workshop did. But there is also a darker meaning: the dreadfully modest hope of living until, and through, summer.

The wildflowers at the quarry's edge may nod to Wallace Stevens's poem "A Postcard from the Volcano," with its poignant evocation of human seasons, memory, and belatedness. I also think of the flower "*tactus aratro*," touched by the plough, which is the final image in Catullus's ragingly sorrowful farewell poem to Lesbia, where sweeping emotions and grandiose geography narrow astonishingly to the precise image of the single doomed flower. Even if the flower appears in the poem only to be lopped down, it is the image of the flower we carry away:

> Tell her not to expect my love any more
> And that it is through her fault that it has fallen
> Like a flower at the edge of a meadow
> When the plough passes.

(Catullus XI, tr. C. H. Sisson*)*

An unlikely mood of gratitude breathes through these poems: gratitude for a rich new friendship, for the rediscovery of some of my own past, and—harder to express—for the reclaiming of the human scale in the only time we can live in, the present. It was as if I was freshly immune to all sorts of current—not only millennial—cant.

That living in the present means, among other things, having access to one's own past was something the workshop proved over and over, the lesson driven home on the scale of individual lives. I'm not sure, but I suspect that the same human scale which millennial rhetoric blows out of all proportion is also obscured or negated by the kind of polarizing language and imagination that has characterized so much of the discourse about AIDS. The talk of "us" versus "them," and of "their" being a marginal and necessarily doomed cohort, disrupts our sense of the tragic continuity of our human situation.

Being human, of course, means that we can only perceive this situation singly, individually, personally, through encounters, feelings, memories. But if we begin on the human scale, individual experiences are apt to take on new dimensions. In "Fin de Siècle," the wildflower epitomizes the summer Charles is hoping for, and hence his hopes themselves. Beyond that, it takes little effort to see the flower on the edge of something cold, deep, and dark as a symbol for Charles; and beyond that, aren't we all flowers at the edge of a quarry? A couple of dreams come back to me at this point. In one, not water but time was flowing through irrigation channels. In the other dream, around the time of my fortieth birthday, there was a vivid image of a steeply sloping deck, at an angle as drastic as that of the sinking *Titanic.* Up and down the deck, harried figures were rushing. The precarious slope was our usual place of business; it was where we lived, all on the edge, all in the same boat.

Half in Love

To scrutinize the future like a sunset!

When I try to get you down on paper
it is as if a sultry film of gold
mists my eyes, and I give in. I put
down the pen and sigh against a sofa,
I lean against a column by the sea
where someone wearing your bright livery
(apricot; azure) smiles in reference
to what, already known,
cannot enter there as a surprise,
may loom or threaten, but is likelier
to blow, an uninvited gust of tedium,
into the marble-pillared hall where, nestled
in knowledge as in folds of coppery satin,
lapped in remembrances, you lie waiting.

The title here is taken from the well-known lines in Keats's "Ode to a Nightingale," "Darkling I listen, and for many a time / I have been half in love with easeful death." It's tempting but probably incorrect to think that the attraction toward unconsciousness expressed in these lines resulted from Keats's knowledge of his own illness. We can find a similar mood of luxurious drowsiness in the "Ode to Indolence." In any case, "Half in Love" can hardly be the first contemporary poem to associate Keats's lines, whatever their precise provenance, with AIDS. A less well-known quote from Keats, it should be noted, expresses the opposite of a wish to die:

> I wish for death every day and night to deliver me from these pains, and then I wish death away, for death would destroy even those pains which are better than nothing. Land and sea, weakness and decline are great seperators [sic], but death is the great divorcer for ever.

As excerpted in this title, though, "half in love" is ambiguous: *who* is half in love, and in love with death or another person? Or is the other person death? Yet no sooner are these alternatives posed than they seem irrelevant. More than love, the poem deals with knowledge. Knowledge takes two forms here, foresight ("to scrutinize the future") and memory ("what, already known, cannot enter . . . as a surprise"). Between these two kinds of knowledge the poem seems paralyzed. Alarmingly for this writer, the wish to "get you down on paper" is baffled;

is dumbness victorious after all? Instead of black and white, there is only a gold mist, and "I give in. I put/down the pen." Oblivion hasn't quite won; the poem, after all, has been written down at some point. But a sense prevails of the stale and superfluous. Nothing is newsworthy any longer, nothing is worth the trouble of telling. Either the subject or language itself has lost its power to surprise, and is likely to blow "an uninvited gust of tedium" into the scene.

The figure who waits at the end of the poem, "nestled/in knowledge as in folds of coppery satin," recalls "The Solarium," where coppery images also iconize a living figure into radiant myth. The process is troubling, and the image of the poet who tries "to get you down on paper" as an uninvited gu[e]st isn't pleasant either. Neither side comes out of this poem very well. It's as if a dialogue is faltering; there is nothing left to say.

One lesson of "Half in Love," with its odd combination of social discomfort and marble halls, is that as intimacy develops, bad moods or just blanknesses can be passed back and forth like a virus. Perhaps I, who languidly "give in . . . put down the pen and sigh against a sofa," am obscurely or not so obscurely mimicking illness, luxuriating in the sense of being too weak to put anything into words any more. Perhaps the figure against the sofa wants to be the center of attention, a position reserved for "you," who "nestled in knowledge . . . lapped in remembrances . . . lie waiting." Passive and omniscient, this figure cannot be surpassed in either weakness or strength.

The ambivalences at play in "Half in Love" can be detected in the chiasmus traceable through the poem's first and last lines, "To scrutinize the FUTURE like a SUNSET" and "lapped in REMEMBRANCES, you lie WAITING." "Future" and "waiting" seem to point ahead; "sunset" and "remembrances" back. Arranged in a square, the four words form an X at whose center we can locate both the vanishing point of the present moment and human consciousness, where even the future has a sunset glow and where what one waits for is already known or remembered.

Baudelaire's "Invitation au Voyage," a more important source than Keats for "Half in Love," similarly mingles future and past in a way that almost annihilates the present. The very word "invitation," like the summons to "imagine," beckons the reader onward toward a fantasized future event and place. Yet the poet actually evokes this place in terms of endings and memories, from the sun setting on the canals to the landscape "which resembles you." In fact all our dreams of the future are conditioned by the past, but in "Half in Love" all such dreams seem, disconcertingly, too well known to need further telling. The poet is in danger of becoming superfluous, and the figure at the finish is oppressed, like the glum young prince in Baudelaire's "Spleen II," by boredom.

The Green Wall

My Dear One is mine as mirrors are lonely.
—W. H. Auden, "The Sea and the Mirror"

I

One is a child and clings and slowly grows
up and detaches, finds another home.
A rooted love undoes itself partway,
waves and wavers, finding a new place
to rest, not too familiar or too strange.
Once these fresh attachments become firm,
daintily they disengage themselves,
lodgers looking for another room.

The sense of life still clasping in her vast
secretive lap some last new thing in store . . .
You waltzed down banks and boulevards, you waited
listening in the garden
for some rumor from the capital.
I chased down sunsets in the river streets
in search of what for all I knew
would be a mocking ghost or even less:
your name, not yet forgotten, on my lips.

II

City of longing! Over the last
barrier to leap, looselimbed,
careless, and dance—a cat, a shadow—down
the avenue of evening,
arcades of circumstances and delights
winking, the promises of veils and awnings,
eyes shut, feeling the heat.
In each doorway luminous phantoms rose,
old adorings, love's biographies,
until it all was parcelled out, bestowed,
clasped and coupled. Nobody was left
at the green limit of your years in leaf.
All the noises finally died away,
leaving doomed occasions still in sight
deserted over the wall.

True, I was there, wondering and watching.
Doomed to be drawn to you,
I balanced on my own
border of late affection,
whose special sunlight, sharp and wintry, brushed
my opaque indoor skin
as an unseeing hand might cup a late
apple only once, then let it hang.

Don't ask me. Poised on my precarious height
I might shout down the news:

I am in love. I am in
the country of lost glimpses.
I feed on death until my eyes are full
and set out, satiated at the start,
for the phantasmagoric marketplace
of dreams in flesh, and go in search of you.

III

I stride the avenues with your name on my lips.
If we should look directly
into the eyes of all who cross our path,
whose dearest wishes would we spy
imprinted there? What secret
stamped on the lids in fire?

Of one's several selves no face is turned
sunlike directly toward the flower of need.
In any instant's path no two attentions
exactly coincide—or if they do,
their countless tiny tendrils freeze together,
locked in a moment's mutuality.

So one persona snarls at an approaching
well-wisher; one shyly turns away
from neutral greetings; still a third (all ready
longingly to lean toward your distant
sunlight) before she's foiled by absence nearly
topples against an invisible pane.

IV

All silken comforts my imagination
concocted for you. Indoors, luxury.
Outdoor scenes let memory supply:
bird sanctuary, rampant vegetation,

and overhead those strangely smiling skies.
Hospital sunsets shed a rosy glow
as far as where I sat (was the source you?)
so bright I finally had to shade my eyes

as if you were a desklamp shining on
scratched clues—the kind one sees by riffling back
through undeciphered sheaves of white and black,
a life unfolded and set partly down.

Blueprints fail to touch upon the future.
I thought the text was one of love and trust,
but as I read a swirl of golden mist
muffled the lines and washed me back to nature.

V

The dream of escape?
                           I have to kindle it.
Wait. I remember there is no escape.
The marriage web we lie in like a hammock
creaks and betrays.
                           I saw an iron life
husked to scaffolding, so sun shone in
on perfect pattern. As flesh flushes red
translucent fruit, this line of years spelled steel.
Then the full moon picked out fingerprints
along the sill. If other shapes could still
emerge from the old efforts of the sun,
what wan familiarities might form?
They stand there in the cold as I lean back,
weight low in the frayed hammock.
It creaks, it cracks: words shaped by one long breath
out of a now dead mouth.
Again my father speaks to me, but neither
waking nor in dreams,
rather skimming the train of the possible

whose sleep-steel-greyish roadbed runs already
far beyond the guesses of becoming.

That scaffolding, though, trembles
like the Condemned Warehouse
I gave my son at Christmas,
designed to be dismantled in advance,
detonated at the flick of a switch
and patiently put back and back together
over and over at an infant whim.

Marriage: cathedral of the unfinished.

VI

The city's speed and flux,
its whitenings, like hair,
and steady gaze, now blurred
as wisps of old desire
speak against the wind,
soften the sting of air.

Allow me to unearth
this pain, this mortal part
and lay the rest to bed,
ease the absence peering
in over the treetops,
gilding the ardent lover
instead of simple sun.

I waited for the sea-green
glow of your gaze to turn
landward at last again
so desperate occasions
could modulate themselves
down to a honey-warm
grumbling in the dark.

VII

Reach above the blanket of an instant
to give it voice. Believe the power will come,
dialogic and reliable
breath of enveloping. Underneath the night
muffle of silence hides this second chance:

if not to say then to put on a saying,
if not to be voiced then to borrow voices
and find what the dull sky was all this while
hiding: what speculation, what loss.

It was as if we looked beyond the wall,
as if we pried beyond the sky's pale panel
to see what waited there. And what we saw
was veiled, not with one veil.

VIII

How to patrol the losses of my days?
Since I never see enough of you,
longing finds an elsewhere—pigeons looped
across the sky, a fleetingly remembered
dream, whatever afternoon can hold to.
Yet what I see—no, dip a finger in—
when we're together is an azure cloud,
radiant, closed. Sometimes the surface breaks
open in a sudden shaft of sunlight
conjured by reminiscences, descriptions,
summoned strengths of what has come and gone.
As for the present, there is a calm pool,
a walk in single file, and a green wall.

IX

It was as if affection finally spoke
out of spring's vague grey-green
skein; or as if many separate
wearinesses gave way to the one rock
against which I could rest—or if not rest,
could sense the deep world shift beneath my feet
and know whatever inner tunnel shivered
crumbling to showers of red gritty dust,
there would be further still to fall, to feel.

You have—I know it—had to give up more.
A cold breeze, hopeful, fitful as the future
keens against the galleries of evening.
Dancer's pose: you lounge against a railing.

Under the arch of death
we met, and only one could pass on through.
Encoded rules said Here is separation.

X

Beautiful waif alarmed into the dark,
your face became my watermark of winter
and then of spring, the poured translucency,
skin, blood, light, an alabaster globe
opened involuntarily
to all the joys and fluids,
the nutrients and poisons of this world.

What shocks it into focus,
this bloom, this blossom
that leaps along the edge,
gulps the breath of every sweet second?
Door, cave, tunnel—more new chambers open,
red, dangerous. Fresh losses
cancel themselves in time.
Something wild is charging
against the wall of spring.

An editor friend to whom I showed "The Green Wall," completed in early June of 1990, wrote that he "envied the life behind it all." This comment pleased me insofar as it meant the poem had succeeded in conveying some of the longing, joy, and energy of a friendship that stayed alive throughout the winter and spring. It also choked me with its (presumably unintended) irony, for what was there to envy in a friendship which seemed to have no future and almost no present?

The answer is, of course, that whether or not it succeeds in transcending its occasion, "The Green Wall" constructs a present by snatching and then building on material from absence. This way of working is said by Northrop Frye in his *Words with Power* to be the way poetry operates in general:

> love poetry, and perhaps all poetry, is the child of the frustration of identity, a presence taking the place of or substituting for an enforced absence.

"Frustration of identity," "enforced absence," "love poetry and perhaps all poetry," are ideas that seem strikingly applicable not only to "The Green Wall" and the other poems addressed to Charles, but also to every other poem here.

I think of a wonderfully Janus-faced phrase my father used to use (did he invent it?) of unsatisfactory books he had to review: "This book (or manuscript, or article) fills a much-needed gap." If I can hold onto this image while smoothing out the puckers of its irony, I think that something like a much-needed gap is what Frye is telling us poetry exists to fill. Unless the gap of absence is there, poetry—that willing presence—has no place to go, no need to fulfill.

The ten sections of "The Green Wall" are ten ways of bridging that gap—ten takes on absence, loss, frustration, quest, dream, disappointment, separation, affection, and hope. They touch on my life as wife and mother, on memories of childhood, on fantasies of striding down city streets. They draw on Charles's own infrequent but always memorable workshop poems, which were the source of the evening scene in Part II and the bird sanctuary in IV. The hospital sunsets in IV glance, of course, at "The Solarium," and the end of VIII echoes that of "Fin de Siècle."

Insofar as it's a medley of motifs from the other poems in this collection, "The Green Wall" can be regarded as a summation. But since what's being summed up is at least as much written or read as lived experience, "The Green Wall" persistently depicts life in terms of written notation and its interpretation and study,

> as if you were a desklamp shining on
> scratched clues—the kind one sees by riffling back
> through undeciphered sheaves of white and black,
> a life unfolded and set partly down.

As in "Half in Love," there is an ambiguous space between the past ("clues" to be "deciphered") and future. Past records prove inadequate:

> Blueprints fail to touch upon the future.
> I thought the text was one of love and trust,
> but as I spoke a swirl of golden mist
> muffled the lines and washed me back to nature.

At one point in the sequence, Frye's "frustration of identity" takes the form of an attempt to pass the ball to the silent person being so persistently addressed. It's *your* turn to talk, to write:

> Reach above the blanket of an instant
> to give it voice . . .
> if not to say then to put on a saying,
> if not to be voiced then to borrow voices

Yet, as if "The Green Wall," and with it all the other poems gathered here, knows it is finally a monologue, the epigraph, from Auden's "The Sea

142

and the Mirror,"glances at the bafflingly reflexive nature of affection—the possibility that when we look at the beloved it is our own face we see. There are assuredly other ways of reading this line, which is part of Miranda's villanelle in Auden's version of *The Tempest*; but I am haunted by a student's comment years ago upon reading both the Shakespeare and Auden. Miranda, this young woman said, was raised without a mirror.

The Sleeping Beauty

Husk of a person beyond summer's pale,
the sleeping beauty dreaded to be woken
even by affection. The moon's veil
shrouded what little sky high monuments
(overgrown themselves by brambles) let
filter through. The spells had all been spoken.
Was it cruel or merciful to move
even a finger closer to the still
deeply breathing figure on the dais,
in slumber royal and illegible?

> Under layers of dust I glimpsed your face.
> As if our year of stories had alighted
> on those shut lips and would at the right word
> emerge and fly into the common air,
> I bent: to catch a signal? steal a kiss
> never in the first place mine to take?
> Was I there to give or to receive?
> As soon as I approached, you seemed to stir,
> as who should ward off a too early waking.
> A pulse like hope beat blood into your cheeks.

The cornered moon shed greyish gleams of dim
illumination down—or transformation?
What would he do or say if he awoke?
Given new life, what would he become?
As I watched, the momentary motion
subsided, and the dream began again,
blanketing him for another year,
another hundred years, when he might wake
(sunlight and breakfast and the table set)
tuned to a kiss still drying on his lips—

> a kiss of friendship and a key to freedom,
> expanse of future, time's apportionment
> to ordinary mornings, noons, and nights.
> All this lay in the world of slender chances
> suspended from a filament of breath
> severed each second by the blade of danger.
> Say you slept a hundred years, then woke

cured but bewildered to an empty world
to take your chances in, with years to spare.
I kiss you. Cured: the word hangs there like smoke.

The penultimate poem here, "The Sleeping Beauty" copes with the problem of self and other by alternating between the third person (stanzas one and three) and the second person (stanzas two and four) so that it's both a small narrative and a personal address. Put another way, "The Sleeping Beauty" twice interrupts its archetypal fairy-tale scenario (though in this version the genders of the one who sleeps and the one who bestows a kiss are reversed) with the thoughts of the person who bends over the sleeper. The kiss which ushers in the happy ending of the traditional version makes an appearance in both the poem's voices; indeed, the kiss ends the poem, but resolution is suspended. For a happy ending in this case would be a cure, and the very word *cured* "hangs there like smoke," an intangible possibility lingering in the air.

The reference to a cure echoes both a poem of Charles's and one of mine. In his "Thirteen Things about a Catheter," stanza XI reads:

> The dream.
> Finally well,
> Over me lies his arm;
> The hole in my chest a lip-smudge,
> Sealed, stamped.

And section IX of my poetic sequence "The Fields of Sleep" (published in *Pass It On* in 1989) quotes my son on the Grimm version:

> Her finger pricked, the Sleeping Beauty fell
> asleep for a hundred summers
> as a result of which (the child
> dabbing the spindle red
> adds) she felt much better.

That is, my son, then aged about three, saw the long sleep not as spell or curse but as cure—something like Hamlet's consummation devoutly to be wished. Death as sleep, then, and sleep as cure, so death as cure?

Death isn't mentioned in "The Sleeping Beauty." The "consummation devoutly to be wished" is merely the resumption of ordinary life, "sunlight and breakfast and the table set." After the long nightmare-ridden sleep of illness, life is morning.

By performing the gesture of the kiss, "The Sleeping Beauty" tries, I suppose, to conjure a cure; but as utterance the poem works more like a wish than a spell. Its mood is echoed in the conclusion of the Larry Josephs article which I have referred to before: "You see, there is nothing I can do about it. Except hope, and dream, and wait." Is the tone here stoically resigned or simply angry? Part of the power of the passage is that it's hard to tell; Josephs won't simplify what is not simple. "The Sleeping Beauty" is prevailingly wistful; it makes no bold claims for the power of devotion to break the spell of illness, but neither does it wholly slam the door on love, even if the object of that love is submerged and unattainable.

"The Sleeping Beauty" nearly ends this group of poems; and as I approach the end of my commentary, I'm aware of two dangers all the poems, as well as what I've said about them, may avoid only narrowly if at all. The simpler danger to diagnose, if not to treat, is the kind of sentimentality I see in "The Lenten Tunnel," which declares there is a light where none may in fact exist. ("The Sleeping Beauty" avoids this particular form of Pollyanna-ishness, but may fall into others.) The other danger is a more complex, and hence a more difficult to describe, form of sentimental wish-fulfillment. It could be put like this: is it an illusion that these poems reach out ? Am I really only mirror-gazing, entranced by my own face? Is the "something wild . . . charging against the wall of spring" in "The Green Wall" perhaps nothing other than my own energy and will? Did all these poems erupt in isolation from the facts, let alone the needs, of the people I was—or thought I was—dealing with? This more subtle and dangerous form of falsity is likelier to seep into poems which address themselves apostrophically toward another, for the illusion of intimacy can both shape and be shaped by a dangerously seductive lyric mode which soars on nothing but its own eloquence.

The last poem here, "Hospitals," avoids such danger by eschewing apostrophe: it is a monologue, almost a mumble.

Hospitals

My new friend finds buffets and matinees and brunches
confusing, but nothing confuses me.
So long as I can swoop through city streets,
life or death, I take it all in stride.
I sift my dreams, those labyrinths of loss,
for figures garbled, recognized, forgotten;
the roulette wheel spins, the Rosetta stone
yields its instructions. For example: Visit
hospitals! And I do, I do, I do,
and having flung my jacket to the floor
and settled down to sweat
in the medicinal and fetid heat,
I sit beside the bed,
make conversation
with temporary faces; and may pluck
some played-out flowers
from their plastic vase
and toss them in the trash
before I plunge back out
and down into the current of the street.

Nothing confuses me.
I tick the hospitals
off on my fingers, see?
Cabrini: eyes of the blackclad saint
strategically located
to focus on each pillow's sweating freight.
St. Vincent's: the same room
where I saw T. in June
K. died in in September.
Co-op Care, where January sunset
gilded the winter river,
lives moving out to sea,
so many and so many
names months prognoses, light
insistent at this window or that window.
September: the school picnic
coincides with K's memorial.
No conflict here: of course

life must prevail. But wait:
picnic or memorial: which is life?

Nothing confuses me.
I hold the categories separate,
see, in the palm, of my hand.
This is the church, this is the steeple.
This is the Cathedral Close.
This is the stoneyard.
Here was the school picnic,
just across the street
from St. Luke's Hospital.
And over there on Broadway
is that not my mother?
Shades walk familiar streets,
facsimiles of faces, of whole bodies.
I recognize the closed
in and the departed,
not ghosts, not lost, but bled
dry of the wound of living.
Nothing confuses me.
I note the tragic mantle
settling in its folds;
I note the body losing,
that same body
which strolled the streets of noon,
telling stories, saying what to do
while daylight lasted. Time
rocks on its haunches, huge
machine I walk through blinking,
tunnel I soon manage not to see;
and while I am not seeing
nothing confuses me.
Hospital and picnic
sit side by side in one
slant of September sun
yet something else is moving,
pressing against the wall of afternoon.
I spread my blanket out on the green lawn.
Winter is coming on.

Written in December 1990 and January 1991, "Hospitals" draws on notes from earlier in the fall of '90, but its immediate occasion was my mother's hospitalization before Christmas for cancer surgery. Briskly enumerating the various Manhattan hospitals with which I had become familiar, "Hospitals" flaunts my implied courage, energy, and clear-headedness while at the same time undermining them. The opening was triggered by my amusement at a friend's claim that she was muddled by marginal occasions like brunch. If a mere hybrid meal threw her off, I thought, how on earth could she deal with the complexities of a life like mine, weaving deftly between zones of life and death?

Luckily I caught the boastfulness of my own thoughts. "Hospitals" begins in a hectoring tone, but soon begins to collapse under the weight of its own repeated assertions: whether in space or in time, what is carefully separated refuses to stay separate. Ostensibly, "Hospitals" takes pride in not connecting, but it ends by conceding that something is on the move—something less nubile than the energy charging at the end of "The Green Wall," something altogether more wintry.

By loudly proclaiming that "nothing confuses me," "Hospitals" both admits my pain and confusion and opens up the possibility of (in Robert Frost's famous words about poetry) a momentary stay against confusion. Confronting the continuity of the memorial service and the picnic is one way to see the two occasions on one plane. I couldn't attend both at once, but they fit harmoniously into a single poem—a poem which claims "I am not seeing," yet which in fact permits me to see the essential structures of a life more clearly.

"Hospitals," a poem which protests too much on purpose, is one more testimony in this collection to the power of language to clarify—a clarification which becomes apparent as "the closed/in and the departed" rise to the surface of vision and the boastful claims subside. The hot air of the repeated "nothing confuses me" is dissipated by the cool autumnal breath of the picnic—or the memorial. All we can do is spread our blankets out for warmth.

It strikes me now that the workshop with its unending dialogue was both a picnic and a memorial, both a feast and a wake. Instead of a blanket on the grass, we had a table in a basement, and there was little to eat except poetry, but in our urban pastoral this frugal entertainment seemed to suffice. I can still hear the chorus of voices:

Sometimes fighting isn't enough . . . a dark cloud hangs over the countryside, everyone asking 'What is it?' . . . Finally well, over me lies his arm . . . Our issue from birth is confidence . . . i spring like violets . . . We feel almost as if we could rule the void . . . Down hospital hallways are heard the lingering fights between the quick and the dead . . . My space is sketched by an unseen cartoonist . . . I'm your new partner, Bed . . . This poet has no rage inside his borrowed cage.

And, finally, I hear Jane Cooper's attestation that in human exchanges something can be made, and then offered, from nothing. Equal in our empty-handedness, we can still give each other gifts:

Conversation by the Body's Light

Out of my poverty
Out of your poverty
Out of your nakedness
Out of my nakedness
Between the swimmer in the water
And the watcher of the skies

Something is altered
Something is offered
Something is breathed
The body's radiance
Like the points of a constellation
Beckons to insight
Here is my poverty:
A body hoarded
Ridiculous in middle age
Unvoiced, unpracticed

And here is your poverty:
A prodigality
That guts its source
The self picked clean
In its shining houses

Out of my nakedness
Out of your nakedness
Between the swimmer in the skies
And the watcher from the water
Something is reached
For a moment, acknowledged
Lost—or is it shelter?
The still not-believed-in
Heartbeat of the glacier

ABOUT THE AUTHOR

Rachel Hadas is the author of several books of poetry, most recently *Pass It On*. Her book *Living in Time*, poetry and memoirs, was published in 1990. Among her awards are a Guggenheim Fellowship in poetry and an award in literature from the American Academy and Institute of Arts and Letters. Hadas is an associate professor of English at Rutgers University. She lives in New York City.